LET'S GO WITH THE CHILDREN

2006

Your passport to fun

RESEARCHED BY ALEX DODGSHON

The only single information source to provide you with comprehensive information about where to take your children in this area.

Children are happier when they are stimulated and occupied and so will *you* be.

This guide makes it easy *for you* to find the right place at the right time and offers you choice to suit not only everyone's interests, but also your pocket.

There are amazing facilities around you which can be fabulous and fun, factual or fantastic and which are quite often *free*.

Check out the chapters to find somewhere to go, or dip into the Sports and Leisure section if you want to be active!

Let us know if you would like this guide to include additional things or if you would like to join our mailing list.

www.letsgowiththechildren.co.uk
Telephone: 01252 322771
Email: enquiries@cubepublications.co.uk

ON THE COVER

02
03
07

THINGS TO DO LOCALLY

Packed with ideas for a new activity or a new hobby, get up, out and active

PLACES TO GO LOCALLY

Within each county area places are grouped into colour coded subjects:

FARMS, WILDLIFE & NATURE PARKS
take a closer look at the animal kingdom

HISTORY, ART & SCIENCE
step back in time, visit a gallery or discover science

FREE PLACES
save money, go somewhere free. (Although free admission, there may be car parking charges, requests for donations or extra charges for special activities)

TRIPS & TRANSPORT
hire a boat, take a train ride and more

ADVENTURE, FUN & SOFT PLAY
fun, play, rides & thrills. Height and age restrictions apply in soft play centres

FURTHER AFIELD

4th Edition

ISBN 1 903594 67 7

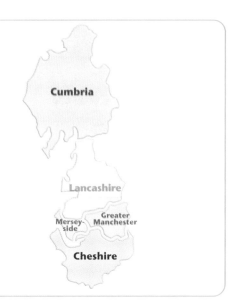

Cumbria

Lancashire

Mersey-side   Greater Manchester

Cheshire

Colour Coding

Each county in this edition is colour coded as shown on this map.

Within each chapter the county areas and town names are colour coded in the same way so you always know where you are. Use this guide with a good geographical map. Let your children help with the map reading. It will open up another world of adventure!

TEAM

EDITING TEAM

Lin Cooksley and Jill Taylor

COVER & IMAGE DESIGN

Ted Evans

PRODUCTION & DESIGN

Karen Martin

ADVERTISING TEAM

Lynda Chantler, Yo Green, Sue Pilgrim, Janet Preston, Emma Rayner, Sue Roberts, Jo Swatland, Ros Walker

PRINTED BY

Pims Print

PUBLISHED BY

Cube Publications
1 Cross Street
Aldershot GU11 1EY

 The History of Great Ormond Street Hospital

Great Ormond Street Hospital for Children (GOSH) opened its doors on 14 February 1852. At the time it was the only centre for children's health in the country and had just 20 beds. Today the hospital is a world-renowned centre of excellence and treats over 90,000 sick children every year. Old buildings constantly need upgrading and a major redevelopment scheme started in 2002. It will see one third of the existing site rebuilt, as well as the creation of some new facilities that will be dedicated to various aspects of modern care for children and resulting in a 20% increased capacity.

Redevelopment Plans

Great Ormond Street Hospital Children's Charity (GOSHCC) is aiming to raise £150 million over the next five years in order to fund the first stages of the hospital's redevelopment. This money will also go towards funding the most up to date equipment; supporting research into and the development of new and better treatments and providing accommodation and other support services for families and staff (GOSHCC accommodates 1,000 parents a week so that they can be near their sick children).

How we can help

We are proud to announce that a 6p contribution will be made for each 'Let's Go with the Children' guide sold this season. This year the funds will go towards equipping the Plaster Room and other areas in the new Orthopaedics Centre.

You can get involved in other ways to help fund raise for GOSHCC. Check out www.gosh.org or call 0207 916 5678 for information

Registered Charity Number: 235825 ©1989 GOSHCC

Key

Price codes are given as a maximum entry cost for a family of four, (2 adults, 2 children):

A	up to £10	
B	up to £20	Please check individual terms and conditions for age definition and number of children on a family ticket
C	up to £30	
D	up to £40	
E	up to £50	
F	FREE	
G	Over £50	
P	Pay as you go	

Schools   Special educational facilities for schools and groups are welcome.

Groups   Facilities for group visits, including schools.

Birthdays   Birthday parties are organised.

School and Group visits and Birthday Parties are by arrangement and often run all year outside stated opening times. Please enquire.

Refreshments There is an eating area and food is available. This may range from a simple snack to a full restaurant meal. Please check in advance so you know what to expect.

V   A money-off voucher is available for this attraction. See Money-off Voucher page.

NT   National Trust property www.nationaltrust.org.uk

EH   English Heritage property www.english-heritage.org.uk

RSPB   Royal Society for the Protection of Birds www.rspb.org.uk

SPECIAL FACILITIES
Should you require special facilities for someone with a disability, please call in advance to check suitability.

OPENING TIMES are included when known at the time of going to print. Please check in advance of your visit if times are not given.

LAST ADMISSIONS are often an hour or more before the quoted closing time.

SCHOOL HOLIDAYS vary around the country and the phrase 'school hols' is a local definition.

WINTER AND CHRISTMAS OPENING
Many attractions close earlier in winter and most are closed over Christmas and New Year.

How to Save Money

Keeping the children entertained doesn't have to be expensive. There are plenty of ways you can save money and enjoy great days out for free!

Use the money saving offers!
- *Check out the Money-off Voucher page and the advertisements.*
Save money on admission prices. For example save up to £25 on a family visit to Legoland. Save up to £29 on a trip to Chessington World of Adventures, or get a whole day for free if you go to Disneyland Paris. Save on your shopping too – £5 off when you shop in Adams Kids stores.
There is lots more! See inside.

Check out the 'Free Places' chapter
- History is fun and often free as many museums are free to enter. Modern museums offer interactive and interesting child-friendly exhibitions. There are country parks, town parks, unusual and surprising places that are all free to go to. Look at the 'Free Places' chapter in this book to find out what is available locally.

Go and be Active
- Use the Sport & Leisure chapter for ideas or just get involved in 'Everyday Sport'. Sport need not be expensive and it is so good to channel all the surplus energy.

Explore the Countryside for free
- Get out into the countryside for trail laying, picnicking, bird watching, animal tracking, fossil collecting, camping, cycling, kite flying, tracking, orienteering, map reading, discovering archaeo-logical sites, or just walking. Give your children the challenge to find a river walk or a hill walk for a great view. You will need a good map which shows lots of detail and all the footpaths.
- Most beaches offer hours of entertainment and exploration. Check out the best ones!
- If it is raining, kit up - there is no weather condition that adequate clothing and equipment can't help with. Tramping in the rain can be fun, but do get some good boots and wet weather gear.

Plan ahead
- Good planning will save you money. Know where you are going, plan your meals out, use the money-saving offers and mention this guide.

HAVE A GREAT DAY OUT!

Snapshots of places to go

Staircase House p57

Smithills Open Farm p51

Chestnut Centre, Otter, Owl & Wildlife Park p81

Sellafield Visitors Centre p42

Please mention this guide when visiting attractions.

Docker Park Farm Visitor Centre p62

Hat Works p55

Redhouse Farm p49

Mersey Ferries p75

For great kids fashion all year round come to adams kids

CONCERT, EXHIBITION & MAJOR EVENT VENUES

GREATER MANCHESTER: Manchester: **Carling Apollo** 08709 913 913, **G-Mex/MICC** 0161 834 2700, **MEN Arena** 0870 190 8000, **National Cycling Centre** Manchester Velodrome Stuart St 0161 223 2244, **National Squash & Athletics Centre** Rowsley St 0161 220 3800.

LOCAL COUNCILS

The Leisure Services Departments of local councils manage a wide range of leisure facilities, from the best parks and open spaces to sports facilities and museums. They may be able to provide further information on special events and playschemes organised for children, particularly in the school holidays.

CHESHIRE: Cheshire County Council: 01244 602424. Chester: 01244 324324. Congleton: 01270 763231. Crewe and Nantwich: 01270 537777. Ellesmere Port and Neston: 0151 356 6789. Halton: 0151 424 2061. Macclesfield: 01625 500500. Vale Royal: 01606 862862. Warrington: 01925 444400.

CUMBRIA: Cumbria County Council: 01228 606060. Allerdale: 01900 326333. Barrow-in-Furness: 01229 894900. Carlisle: 01228 817000. Copeland: 01946 852585. Eden: 01768 864671. South Lakeland: 01539 733333.

GREATER MANCHESTER: Bolton: 01204 333333. Bury: 0161 253 5000. Manchester: 0161 234 5000. Oldham: 0161 911 3000. Rochdale: 01706 647474. Salford: 0161 794 4711. Stockport: 0161 480 4949. Tameside: 0161 342 8355. Trafford: 0161 912 1212. Wigan: 01942 244991.

LANCASHIRE: Lancashire County Council: 01772 254868. Blackburn with Darwen: 01254 585585. Blackpool: 01253 477477. Burnley: 01282 425011. Chorley: 01257 515151. Fylde: 01253 658658. Hyndburn: 01254 388111. Lancaster: 01524 582000. Pendle: 01282 661661. Preston: 01772 906000. Ribble Valley: 01200 425111. Rossendale: 01706 217777. South Ribble: 01772 421491. West Lancashire: 01695 577177. Wyre: 01253 891000.

MERSEYSIDE: Knowsley: 0151 489 6000. Liverpool: 0151 233 3000. St Helens: 01744 456000. Sefton: 01704 533133. Wirral: 0151 638 7070.

TOURIST INFORMATION CENTRES

Tourist Information Centres are a great complement to this guide. They can provide a personal opinion on many interesting local attractions and one-off events. They also stock colour leaflets about attractions featured in this book.

S/O indicates seasonal opening.

CHESHIRE: Chester: 01244 402111. Congleton: 01260 271095. Knutsford: 01565 632611. Macclesfield: 01625 504114. Nantwich & Upper Weaver Valley: 01270 610983. Northwich: 01606 353534. Runcorn: 01928 576776. Warrington: 01925 632571. Wilmslow: 01625 522275.

CUMBRIA: Alston Moor: 01434 382244. Ambleside: 01539 432582. Appleby-in-Westmorland: 017683 51177. Barrow-in-Furness: 01229 894784. Bowness-on-Windermere: 015394 42895. Brampton: 016977 3433 S/O. Broughton-in-Furness: 01229 716115. Carlisle: 01228 625600. Cockermouth: 01900 822634. Coniston: 015394 41533. Egremont: 01946 820693. Grange-over-Sands: 015395 34026. Grasmere: 015394 35245. Hawkshead: 015394 36525. Kendal: 01539 725758. Keswick: 017687 72645. Killington

Lake: 015396 20138 S/O. Kirby Lonsdale: 01524 271437. Kirkby Stephen: 017683 71199. Maryport: 01900 812101. Penrith: 01768 867466. Pooley Bridge: 017684 86530 S/O. Rheged: 01768 868000. Seatoller: 017687 77294 S/O. Sedbergh: 015396 20125 S/O. Silloth-on-Solway: 01697 331944. Southwaite: 016974 73445. Ullswater: 017684 82414. Ulverston: 01229 587120. Waterhead: 015394 32729 S/O. Whitehaven: 01946 852939. Windermere: 01539 446499. Workington: 01900 606699.

GREATER MANCHESTER: Altrincham: 0161 912 5931. Ashton-under-Lyne: 0161 343 4343. Bolton: 01204 334321. Bury: 0161 253 5111. Manchester: 0161 234 3157. Oldham: 0161 627 1024. Rochdale: 01706 864928. Saddleworth: 01457 870336. Salford: 0161 848 8601. Stockport: 0161 474 4444. Wigan: 01942 825677.

LANCASHIRE: Accrington: 01254 872595. Barnoldswick: 01282 666704. Bentham: 015242 62549. Blackburn with Darwen: 01254 53277. Blackpool: 01253 478222. Burnley: 01282 664421. Cleveleys: 01253 853378. Clitheroe: 01200 425566. Fleetwood: 01253 773953. Garstang: 01995 602125. Lancaster: 01524 32878. Lytham St Anne's: 01253 725610. Morecambe: 01524 582808. Pendle: 01282 661701. Preston: 01772 253731. Rawtenstall: 01706 244678.

MERSEYSIDE: Birkenhead: 0151 647 6780. Liverpool: 09066 806886. St Helens: 01744 755150. Southport: 01704 533333.

Dealing with a bee sting

During a visit to a wildlife centre, a bee stings your son on his hand. The sting is visible in the skin, with a redness and swelling forming around it. What do you do?

Scrape the sting away using a flat object, like a credit card. This will work better than tweezers, which can squeeze more poison into the skin. Once the sting has been removed, apply a cold compress. A bag of frozen vegetables is perfect but, when you're out and about, try an ice-lolly with the wrapper left on. Failing that, pour cold water over the injury.

To learn more about first aid visit redcross.org.uk/firstaid or call 0870 170 9222

First TransPennine Express, *www.tpexpress.co.uk*
Leave the car behind and start a great day out with a First TransPennine Express train journey that is going to be fun for everyone! Frequent services link the major centres from the east coast to the west, offering easy access to the lovely attractions of York and Scarborough, the Pennine Hills, the Lake District and the Victorian heritage of towns and cities from Liverpool to Leeds. There are links with local buses, trams and cycle shops creating a good transport network all the way to the attractions, so getting around is easier than ever. Travelling with First TransPennine Express is fun for children with brand new Carriage Crew Kids Packs available during school holidays on board the trains with catering facilities. These funky rucksacks are packed with postcards and crayons, a jotter pad to spot things along the route and loads of pictures to colour in including an adventure story based on the legendary Tizzie Wizzie creature in the Lake District. So don't forget to ask for your Carriage Crew Kids Packs the next time you have a family day out with First TransPennine Express! For more information and to buy your train tickets online, visit the website above. **Check out outside back cover.**

YOU DON'T HAVE TO SPEND A FORTUNE TO ENTERTAIN THE KIDS.

Have you ever thought of giving your family the run around in the park with a frisbee or a tennis ball?

What about your local leisure centre? You don't have to be a budding David Beckham or Kelly Holmes to go along. There are all sorts of activities to take part in — from family fun to team or extreme.

Getting active can be fun, easy and great for your family's health.

EVERYDAY SPORT

Every body feels better for it.

For ideas on how you can get active and healthy — at home or on holiday — log on to www.everydaysport.com or call 0800 587 6000.

Sports & Leisure

port is a great way for young people to channel surplus energy or occupy spare time. It can offer personal challenge, foster team spirit and generate an interest that can provide a pleasurable and necessary diversion in later life. Sport is a good way to have fun, make new friends, to be fit and feel good. Try climbing, snow sports or the many different activities on offer at your sports and leisure centre. Leisure pursuits may lead to a new hobby or simply occupy leisure time in a relaxed and entertaining way. Try pottery painting, go to the theatre or have a go at ten-pin bowling.

Abbreviations: A: Archery, Ab: Abseiling, AC: Assault Course, B: Bellboating, C: Canoeing & Canoes, CC: Camp Craft, Cl: Climbing, Cv: Caving, DB: Dragon Boating, F: Fencing, GW: Gorge Walking, HW: Hill Walking, K: Kayaking & Kayaks, Kt: Karting, M: Motor Boats, MB: Mountain Biking, Mt: Mountaineering, NB: Narrow Boats, O: Orienteering, PB: Power Boating, Pd: Pedaloes, PS: Problem Solving, Q: Quad Biking, R: Riding, Rf: Rifle Shooting, Ro: Rowing, RsC: Ropes Courses, Rt: Rafting Activities, S: Sailing, SD: Sailing Dinghies, TB: Team Building, Tr: Trapeze, W: Windsurfing & boards, Wb: Wakeboarding, WS: Water Skiing, Z: Zipwire.

ADVENTURE HOLIDAYS

PGL Activity Holidays, www.pgl.co.uk 08700 507 507.
There are 18 different activity holidays for 7-10, 10-13 and 13-16 year olds to choose from, including pony trekking, adrenaline adventure, kayaking, dance and learner driver. They have 10 residential centres and offer escorted travel from towns and cities around the UK. PGL also offer winter sports in Austria, holidays in France and 'Family Active' adventure holidays for all the family. Call 0500 749 147 for a free brochure. **Check out page 12.**

AFTER SCHOOL CLASSES

Kumon Educational, www.kumon.co.uk or freephone 0800 854714.
The Kumon method is about more than Maths and English and promotes a positive, 'can-do' attitude to boost confidence and enhance many aspects of a child's life. The child is shown focus skills designed to enable them to work independently, and within a target time, meaning that they can get more done in exams and school work. A strong focus on the crucial areas of mental arithmetic and times tables, reading and grammar, with a motivational and individual approach to the child's learning experience, has made Kumon successful. There are 540 study centres throughout the UK, so one is usually within easy reach. Thought for the Day from Kumon Instructor Harry Lea-Gerrard, Ashton-under-Lyne: Life is about facing challenges and overcoming them. It's a powerful lesson to learn that if you want to achieve something, it takes a bit of effort. And a little bit of effort every day is better than one big effort once a week or once a month. We let our children down sometimes if we make life too easy for them, or if we let them give up as soon as they find something hard. **Check out inside back cover.**

ART & CRAFT ACTIVITIES

Crafty Kidz, www.craftykidz.net 0845 3700 123.
Paint and create with imaginative art and craft classes for children 12 months to teens. There are messy play sessions for toddlers to experiment and learn through painting, colouring, sticking, playdough, cooking and more, and make as much mess as they like! Saturday classes, after school art and craft workshops, and summer holiday art and craft classes are full of activities that will inspire creativity in children aged 4-14yrs. Book a party co-ordinator to run a craft party (3-14yrs), or buy a party in a box kit online! Birthdays **Check out page 12.**

Messy Monsters, *www.messymonsters.co.uk 0161 798 4518.*
Get messy and have fun at this exciting and educational art club, where children can take part in painting, drawing, collage, playdough and model building in a calm and relaxed environment. There are 1hr classes for 2-4yrs and 45-minute classes for 6months-2yrs, entirely devoted to art, craft and mess with no clearing up afterwards! Each week there is a different theme, with both structured and free play activities and adults are encouraged to join in the fun. Birthdays **Check out page 12.**

ARTS CENTRES

Centres often offer a mix of contemporary galleries and are venues for performing arts, festivals and workshops.
CHESHIRE: Warrington: **Pyramid & Parr Hall** Palmyra Sq South 01925 442345.
CUMBRIA: Kendal: **Brewery Arts Centre** Highgate 01539 725133.
GREATER MANCHESTER: Manchester: **Chinese Arts Centre** Thomas St 0161 832 7271, **Cornerhouse** 70 Oxford St 0161 200 1500. Rochdale: **Skylight Circus Arts** Smith St 01706 650676. Salford: **The Lowry** Salford Quays 0870 787 5780, **Walk the Plank Theatre Ship** 72 Broad St 0161 736 8964.
MERSEYSIDE: Birkenhead: **Pacific Road Arts Centre** Pacific Rd 0151 647 0752. St Helens: **The Citadel** Waterloo St 01744 735436. Southport: **Southport Arts Centre** Lord St 01704 540011.

BOARDING & BMX

Listed here is a selection of the larger centres in the North West. Check with your local council for more skateboard facilities.
CHESHIRE: Chester: **The Boneyard Skatepark** Tattenhall Works Canalside Tatternhall 01829 770771.
GREATER MANCHESTER: Bolton: **Bones Skatepark** Gilnow La Deane 01204 392939. Manchester: **Projekt** Mancunian Way 0161 832 5677. Stockport: **Bones Skatepark** Canal St 0161 480 8118.
LANCASHIRE: Blackpool: **Ramp City WSA** Cropper Rd Marton 01253 699005. Burnley: **Interact Park** Colne St 01282 455363.
MERSEYSIDE: Liverpool: **Rampworx** 1-3 Leckwith Rd Netherton 0151 530 1500.

BOAT HIRE

The key to abbreviations is at the beginning of this chapter.
CHESHIRE: Bunbury: **Anglo Welsh Holidays** 01829 260957 NB. Crewe: **Queens Park** Wistaston Rd Ro. Nantwich: **Nantwich Canal Centre** Basin End 01270 625122 NB. Scholar Green: **Heritage Narrow Boats** The Marina 01782 785700 NB.
CUMBRIA: Ambleside: **Windermere Lake Cruises** 015394 32225 Ro. Borrowdale: **Platty Plus** Lodore Boat Landings 017687 76572 C DB K PB Ro SD. Bowness: **Windermere Lake Cruises** 015394 88178 M Ro. Coniston: **Coniston Boating Centre** Lake Rd 015394 41366 C K M Ro SD. Keswick: **Derwent Water Marina** Portinscale 017687 72912 C K Ro SD W, **Keswick Launch Company** Keswick Boat Landings 017687 72263 M Ro. Newby Bridge: **Fell Foot Park** 015395 31273 Ro. Windermere: **Shepherds** Bowness Bay 015394 45395 M.
GREATER MANCHESTER: Littleborough: **Hollingworth Lake Water Activity Centre** Lakebank 01706 370499 Ro. Oldham: **Alexandra Park** King's Rd Ro. Prestwich: **Heaton Park** Middleton Rd 0161 773 1085 Ro.
LANCASHIRE: Blackpool: **Stanley Park** West Pk Dri 01253 478428 M Pd Ro. Chorley: **L and L Cruises** Heath Charnock 01257 480825 NB. Lytham St Anne's: **Fairhaven Lake** Inner Promenade 01253 725610 C M Ro W.
MERSEYSIDE: Southport: **Marine Lake** The Promenade 01704 539701 M.

Contact details for Megabowl/Tenpin centres are given in the box below.

CHESHIRE: Chester: **Megabowl/Tenpin*** Unit 33 The Greyhound Pk Sealand Rd. Ellesmere Port: **Megabowl/Tenpin*** Coliseum Leisure Pk Coliseum Way. Macclesfield: **AMF Bowling** London Rd 0870 118 3022. New Brighton: **Riverside Bowl & Lazerquest** Marine Promenade 0151 639 1238. Northwich: **Winnington Bowl** Winnington La 01606 786836. Warrington: **LA Bowl** Chetham Court Winwick Quay 01925 639222.

CUMBRIA: Barrow-in-Furness: **Superbowl** Hollywood Pk 01229 820444. Carlisle: **AMF Bowling** Currock Rd 0870 118 3013. Workington: **Eclipse Ten Pin Bowling Centre** Derwent Howe Ind Est 01900 872207.

GREATER MANCHESTER: Bolton: **Hollywood Bowl** 25-27 The Linkway Middlebrook Leisure and Retail Pk Horwich 01204 692999. Bury: **Megabowl/Tenpin*** Park 66 Pilsworth Ind Est. Didsbury: **Megabowl/Tenpin*** Parr Wood Entertainment Centre Wilmslow Rd. Leigh: **Superbowl** Windermere Rd 01942 606731. Rochdale: **Strike Ten Bowl** Sandbrook Retail Pk 01706 638383. Stockport: **Megabowl/Tenpin*** Grand Central Leisure Pk Wellington Rd. Trafford Centre: **Namco Station** The Orient 0161 749 1111. Wigan: **AMF Bowling** Miry La 0870 118 3038. Worsley: **XS Superbowl** 30 Shield Dri Wardley Ind Est 0161 794 3374.

LANCASHIRE: Accrington: **Superbowl** The Viaduct Hyndburn Rd 01254 875500. Blackpool: **Blackpool Superbowl** 29-37 Market St 01253 752020, **Premier Bowl** Blackpool Mecca Buildings Central Dri 01253 295503. Burnley: **AMF Bowling** Finsley Gate 0870 118 3012. Morecambe: **Superbowl** Central Dri 01524 400974. Preston: **Lakeside Superbowl** 50 Greenbank St 01772 555080, **Megabowl/Tenpin*** Capitol Centre Walton-le-Dale. St Anne's: **Surfside Family Amusement Centre** The Island 01253 722666.

MERSEYSIDE: Bootle: **Megabowl/Tenpin*** Switch Island Leisure Pk. Liverpool: **Hollywood Bowl** Edge La Retail Pk 0151 228 1048. Southport: **Premier Bowl** Ocean Plaza Marine Dri 01704 543569.

---

*MEGABOWL/TENPIN: (0871 550 1010) www.megabowl.co.uk/www.tenpin.co.uk

---

IdentiKids, *www.identifyme.co.uk 0845 125 9539.*
It doesn't take long for your child to wander off when you're out and about but it's even quicker to put an IdentiKids wristband on them, for your peace of mind and their safety. Other ID solutions available, including medical and allergy bands. **Check out page 14.**

Lion in the Sun, *www.lioninthesun.com 01483 565301.*
Junior surf brand stocking sun protective swimwear and beach fashions for babies, children, teens and adults. Swimshirts, boardies, UV suits, sun hats and tankinis, all with UPF 50+ for peace of mind at the beach. **Check out page 14.**

Contact details for the large cinema groups are given in the box below.

CHESHIRE: Chester: **Cineworld** Greyhound Retail Pk Sealand Rd, **Odeon** Northgate St. Ellesmere Port: **Vue** The Coliseum. Knutsford: **Studio Knutsford Civic Centre** Toft Rd 01565 633005. Northwich: **Regal** London Rd 01606 43130. Runcorn: **Cineworld** Halton Lea Shopping Centre. Warrington: **UCI** Westbrook Centre.

CUMBRIA: Ambleside: **Zeffirellis** Compston Rd 01539 431771. Barrow-in-Furness: **Apollo** Hollywood Pk 0871 223 3442. Carlisle: **Lonsdale** Warwick Rd 01228 525586, **Vue** 50 Botchergate. Cockermouth: **The Kirkgate Centre** Kirkgate 01900 826448. Kendal: **Brewery Arts Centre** Highgate 01539 725133. Keswick: **Alhambra** St Johns St 01768 772195. Penrith: **Alhambra** Middlegate 01768 862400. Ulverston: **Roxy** Brogden St 01229 582340. Windermere: **Royalty** Lake Rd Bowness 01539 443364. Workington: **Plaza** Maryport Rd Siddick 01900 870001.

GREATER MANCHESTER: Ashton under Lyne: **Cineworld** Fold Way. Bolton: **Cineworld** Eagley Brook Way, **Vue** Middlebrook LC. Bury: **Vue** Park 66 Pilsworth Rd. Didsbury: **Cineworld** Parrs Wood Entertainment Centre Wilmslow Rd. Heaton Moor: **Savoy** Heaton Moor Rd 0161 432 2114. Manchester: **AMC** 253 Deansgate 0870 755 5657, **Cornerhouse** 70 Oxford St 0161 200 1500, **Showcase** Hyde Rd Belle **Vue** 0871 220 1000, **UCI** Filmworks Printworks Centre, **UCI** The Trafford Centre The Dome. Marple: **Regent** Stockport Rd 0161 427 5951. Rochdale: **Odeon** Sandbrook Pk. Salford: **Vue** The Red Cinema Lowry Designer Outlet. Stockport: **Cineworld** Grand Central Sq Wellington Rd South, The Plaza Mersey Sq 0161 477 7779. Urmston: **Curzon** Princess Rd 0161 748 2929. Wigan: **Cineworld** Robin Pk.

LANCASHIRE: Accrington: **Vue** The Viaduct Hyndburn Rd. Blackburn: **Apollo** King William St 0871 223 3446, **Vue** Peel Leisure & Retail Pk Lower Audley St. Blackpool: **Odeon** Rigby Rd. Burnley: **Apollo** Manchester Rd Hollywood Pk 0871 223 3445. Clitheroe: **Grand** York St 01200 427162. Lancaster: **The Dukes** Moor La 01524 598500, **Regal** 71 King St 01524 64141. Lytham St Annes: **Cinema 4 'The Flicks'** Pleasure Island 01253 722620. Morecambe: **Apollo** Central Dri 0871 223 3461. Preston: **The Palace** Longridge Market Pl 01772 785600, **UCI** Riversway, **Vue** The Capitol Centre Walton-le-Dale.

MERSEYSIDE: Allerton: **Odeon** Allerton Rd. Birkenhead: **Vue** Europa Boulevard Conway Pk. Bootle: **Odeon** Switch Island. Bromborough: **Odeon** Welton Rd. Liverpool: **Cineworld** Edge La Retail Pk, **FACT** 88 Wood St 0151 707 4450, **Odeon** London Rd, **Plaza Community Cinema** Crosby Rd North 0151 474 4076, **Showcase** East Lancashire Rd 0871 220 1000. Woolton: **Woolton Cinema** Mason St 0151 428 1919. St Helens: **Cineworld** Chalon Way West. Southport: **Vue** Marine Dri.

CINEWORLD CINEMAS Hotline: 0871 220 8000/0871 200 2000
www.cineworld.co.uk

ODEON CINEMAS Hotline: 0871 22 44 007 www.odeon.co.uk

UCI CINEMAS Hotline: 0871 22 44 007 www.uci.co.uk

VUE CINEMAS Hotline: 0871 22 40 240 www.myvue.com

CLIMBING WALLS

Also check out 'Outdoor Pursuits' as many centres offer outdoor rock climbing.

CHESHIRE: Chester: **The Walls** Unit 7 Chesterbank Business Pk River La Saltney 01244 682626. Warrington: **The North West Face** St Ann's Church Winwick Rd 01925 650022.

CUMBRIA: Barrow-in-Furness: **Park Leisure Centre** Greengate St 01229 871146. Cockermouth: **Cockermouth Leisure Centre** Castlegate Dri 01900 823596. Kendal: **Lakeland Climbing Centre** Lake District Business Pk Mint Bridge Rd 01539 721766. Keswick: **Keswick Climbing Wall** Southey Hill Ind Est 017687 72000. Penrith: **Eden Climbing Wall** Penrith LC Southend Rd 01768 863450.

GREATER MANCHESTER: Manchester: **Manchester Climbing Centre** Bennett St 0161 230 7006. Oldham: **Oldham Sports Centre** Lord St 0161 911 4090. Rochdale: **Balderstone Technology College** Queen Victoria St Balderstone 01706 751500. Stockport: **The Rope Race** Goyt Mill Upper Hibbert La Marple 0161 426 0226.

LANCASHIRE: Blackburn: **Boulder UK** Heaton St 01254 693056. Carnforth: **Inglesport** The Square Ingleton 015242 41146. Clitheroe: **Roefield Leisure Centre** Edisford Rd 01200 442188. Lancaster: **Indoor Climbing Wall** Lancaster University Sports Centre 01524 594000. Rochdale: **Climb** Rochdale School La 01706 524450.

MERSEYSIDE: Liverpool: **Awesome Walls Climbing Centre** St Albans Church Athol St 0151 298 2422.

CYCLE HIRE

CHESHIRE: Knutsford: **Cyclelife** Tatton Pk 01625 534400.
CUMBRIA: Ambleside: **Biketreks** Millans Pk 015394 31505, **Ghyllside Cycles** The Slack 015394 33592. Brampton: **Pedal Pushers Cycle Hire** Sandy Lonning 016977 42387. Cockermouth: **Grin Up North** 01900 829600. Coniston: **Summitreks** Unit 2 Lake Rd 015394 41212. Hawkshead: **Grizedale Mountain Bikes** Grizedale Visitor Centre Grizedale Forest Pk 01229 860369. Keswick: **Keswick Mountain Bikes** Southey Hill 017687 75202. Langwathby: **Cycle Active** 8 Low Mill 01768 840400. Staveley: **Millennium Cycles** Bankside Barn Crook Rd 01539 821167. Windermere: **Country Lanes Cycle Centre** Windermere Railway Station 01539 444544.
LANCASHIRE: Clitheroe: **Pedal Power** Waddington Rd 01200 422066. Lancaster: **Budgie Bikes** Lancaster Railway Station 01524 389410.

GIFTS & PARTY WEAR

Able-Direct, www.able-labels.co.uk 0870 444 2733.
Have your name or personalised message printed, woven, engraved or embroidered onto a huge range of products including mugs, pens and pencils, silverware and labels. You can even personalise one of five children's books so your child becomes the main character in their very own story. Able-Direct will give schools cash back for every item ordered - call for details and an order form, or go to the website to view the full range of products. **Check out page 14.**

Little Mischiefs, *10 Causewayhead Road, Dore, near Sheffield, www.littlemischiefs.co.uk 0114 262 1020.*
Specialists in a wide range of quality children's gifts including personalised keepsakes. Also stockists of Lucy Locket, Fiesta Crafts, Wingreen, Kaloo and more. Shop online at www.littlemischiefs.co.uk. **Check out page 14.**

ICE SKATING

LANCASHIRE: Blackburn: **Ice Arena** Lower Adley 01254 263063. Blackpool: **Pleasure Beach Arena** Ocean Boulevard 0870 444 5566.

KARTING & QUAD BIKING

CHESHIRE: Warrington: **Speed Karting** Unit 2 Bank Quay Trading Est 01925 415114.
CUMBRIA: Carlisle: **Carlisle Indoor Karting** Newtown Ind Est 01228 510061. Maryport: **West Coast Indoor Karting** Solway Trading Est 01900 816472.
GREATER MANCHESTER: Gorton: **Karting 2000** Froxmer St 0161 231 2000. Manchester: **Mud Monsters** 07812 389962. Trafford Park: **Daytona** Unit 4 Circle South Trafford Pk Rd 0161 876 0876. Wigan: **Three Sisters Race Circuit** Bryn Rd Ashton-in-Makerfield 01942 270230, **Wigan Pier Indoor Karting** Swan Meadow Rd 01942 829697.
LANCASHIRE: Blackpool: **Blackpool Karting Centre** Central Dri 01253 292600, **Karting 2000** New South Promenade 01253 408068. Burscough: **Kartworld** Tollgate Rd 01704 896633. Colne: **Prestige Indoor Karting** Holker Mill Burnley Rd 01282 865675. Preston: **Quad Centre Trax** Riverside Pk Wall End Rd Preston Docklands 01772 735734, **Trax Motorsport** Riverside Pk Wall End Rd Preston Docklands 01772 731832.
MERSEYSIDE: Liverpool: **Mersey Indoor Karting** Unit 1 Paragon Centre Picton Rd 0151 734 1736. Southport: **Go Karting** Pleasureland 0870 220 0204.

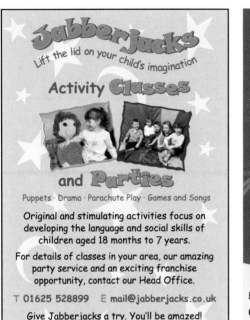

Jabberjacks, *www.jabberjacks.co.uk 01625 528899(head office).*
Inspiring activity classes and party entertainment for children aged 18 months to 7 years. The highly original activities include music, drama, puppets and physical play with the focus on developing children's language and social skills. For information about classes in your area or details about the exciting franchise opportunity available, please telephone or contact via the website. Birthdays **Check out page 18.**

Jo Jingles, *www.jojingles.com 01494 778989.*
A marvellous music and singing experience with an educational slant for children aged 6 months to 5 years (up to 7 & 8 years in some areas). Exciting and stimulating classes run at venues all over the country. For details on classes in your area or for information on the franchise opportunity please call 01494 778989, email: headoffice@jojingles.co.uk or visit the website. Birthdays **Check out page 18.**

Kindermusik, *www.kindermusik.co.uk 01276 62407.*
A leading music and movement programme for children newborn to 7 yrs, reaching over a million children worldwide. Small, fun classes are offered to help develop all aspects of childhood development based on the latest research and endorsed by childhood development experts. Quality teaching and home materials including CDs, books and instruments are provided. **Check out page 18.**

Monkey Music, *www.monkeymusic.co.uk 01582 766464.*
Children's music classes held across the UK. Educational and entertaining, they are led by specialist teachers in an imaginative and social environment. Classes are small and carefully structured, with children from 0-4yrs grouped according to age. Birthdays **Check out page 18.**

For water-based activities also check out 'Watersports'.
The key to abbreviations is at the beginning of this chapter.
CUMBRIA: Coniston: **Summitreks** 14 Yewdale Rd 015394 41212 Ab C Cl GW K HW MB O. Eskdale: **Outward Bound** Eskdale Gr 0870 513 4227 C CC Cl GW K O RsC Rt S Tr. Glenridding: **Patterdale Hall** 017684 82233 A Ab C Cl Cv GW K Mt RsC S. Greenodd: **River Deep Mountain** High Main St 01229 861497 Ab C Cl GW HW K MB Rt. Grizedale: **Go Ape!** Grizedale Forest Visitor Centre 0870 444 5562 RsC. Kendal: **Adventure Days** 28 Finkle St 01539 720750 Ab Cl Cv. Keswick: **Keswick Climbing Wall & Activity Centre** 017687 72000 Ab AC C Cl MB Rt, **Newlands Adventure Centre** Stair 017687 78463 Ab C Cl HW K MB O RsC, **Vivid Events** Penrith Rd 017687 75351 Ab C Cl HW O Rt. Lamplugh: **Carolclimb Outdoor Adventures** Todhole Farm 01946 862746 C Cl GW K Mt O. Penrith: **Rookin House Farm** Troutbeck 01768 483561 AC Kt Q R. Portinscale: **Cumbria Outdoors** Hawse End Centre 017687 72816 A Ab C Cl Cv GW K MB O SD. Staveley: **Adventure Learning** Kendal Rd 01539 821728 C Cl Cv HW. Ullswater: **Howtown Outdoor Centre** 01768 486508 A C Cl GW K SD RsC, **Outward Bound** Watermillock 0870 513 4227 C CC Cl GW K O RsC Rt S Tr. Ulverston: **Water Park Adventure Centre** High Nibthwaite 01229 885456 C Cl HW K O PS RsC S W. Windermere: **Mere Mountains** Keldwyth Pk 015394 88002 Ab C Cl Cv GW K O Rt, **Pleasure in Leisure Ltd** Tirobeck 015394 42324 A Ab C Cl Cv GW Kt O R S, **R & L Adventures** Knots Farm Patterdale Rd 015394 45104 Ab Cl Cv GW HW K O, **Windermere Outdoor Adventure** Rayrigg Rd 015394 47183 C Cl HW K S W.
GREATER MANCHESTER: Bury: **Alternative Adventure** Seddons Farm House Newington Dri 0161 764 3612 A Ab C Cl Cv GW MB O Rt TB, **Burrs Activity Centre** Burrs Country Pk Woodhill Rd 0161 764 9649 A Ab C Cl K O PS Rt. Castleton: **Castleton Water Activity Centre** Maltings La off Manchester Rd 01706 639378 A C Cl F K MB O Rt TB. Manchester: **Debdale Outdoor Centre** Hyde Rd Gorton 0161 223 5182 C Cl K PB SD WS.

LANCASHIRE: Carnforth: **Borwick Hall** Borwick 01524 732508 Ab AC C Cl Cv K MB RsC Rt TB Z. Ormskirk: **Rock and River** Wood La 01704 822644 A Ab C Cl K O PS Rf RsC Rt Tr Z.
MERSEYSIDE: Liverpool: **Merseyside Youth Challenge Trust** Allerton Tower Pk Menlove Ave 0151 428 9758 A Ab CC Cl O RsC Rt. New Brighton: **Elemental Outdoors Ltd** Marine Lake 0151 691 0941 Ab C CC Cl GW K O PS TB.

PAINTBALLING

Paintballing is suitable for older children only. It is popular with some teenagers and adults but it is important that you check out the organisation offering the activity for your children and be satisfied that proper safety regulations are observed. Some of the sites below are members of the United Kingdom Paintball Sports Federation (www.ukpsf.com), but the sport does not appear to be regulated. In all cases, parents should check suitability before booking.
CHESHIRE: Congleton: **Delta Force** Zuluwood Brereton Gr 0800 917 0821. Frodsham: **National Paintball Games** between M6 and M56 0800 072 6969.
CUMBRIA: Penrith: **Bravo 4 Zero** Low Woodside Brougham 01768 88467.
LANCASHIRE: Accrington: **Outdoor Action Pursuits** The Dunkenhalgh Hotel 01282 414407. Bickerstaff: **Delta Force** Minsterwood Nipe La 0800 917 0821. Chorley: **Paintball Experience** 01706 345821. Ormskirk: **Combat Paintball** Firswood Rd Lathom 0151 284 7700. Preston: **Paintball Trax** Wallend Rd off Nelson Way 07811 480660.
MERSEYSIDE: Southport: **Frontline Paintball** Leisure Lakes Mere Brow 0151 928 7696.

Delta Force, *www.paintballgames.co.uk 0800 917 0821.*
Worlds apart from tame indoor laser games, children from the age of eleven will love the genuine thrill of live action paintball scenarios played over large and varied outdoor landscapes. Special events are held regularly. Birthdays **Open all year Check out advert below.**

PITCH & PUTT

CHESHIRE: Chester: **Westminster Park** Hough Gr 01244 680231. Warrington: **Walton Hall Gardens** Higher Walton 01925 601617.
GREATER MANCHESTER: Oldham: **Bishops Park** Grains Bar (Easter-Sept) 0161 633 1635.
MERSEYSIDE: New Brighton: **Kings Parade Gardens** Marine Promenade 0151 606 2000, **Wallasey Beach Mini Golf** Harrison Dri 0151 639 1286. Wirral: **Arrowe Country Park** Arrowe Pk Rd 0151 677 7594.

PONY TREKKING

CUMBRIA: Millom: **Murthwaite Green Trekking Centre** Silecroft 01229 770876.
GREATER MANCHESTER: Birtle: **Birtle & Rochdale Riding School** Higher Elbut Farm Elbut La 0161 764 6573. Littleborough: **Dickey Steps Riding School** Rakewood Rd 01706 373919.
LANCASHIRE: Blackburn: **Warrens Riding Centre** 5 Garsden Ave 01254 57683. Darwen: **Earnsdale Farm Riding School** Duddon Ave 01254 702647.

POTTERY ACTIVITIES

CHESHIRE: Hale Village: **The Art Cafe** Ashley Rd 0161 929 6886. Nantwich: **Firs Pottery** Sheppenhall La 01270 780345. Northwich(near): **Stockley Farm** Arley 01565 777323. Poynton: **Brookside Pottery** Brookside Garden Centre Macclesfield Rd 01625 872919. Sandbach: **The Potters Barn** Roughwood La Hassall Gr 01270 884080.
CUMBRIA: Bowness: **Colourpots** 59 Quarry Rigg Lake Rd 015394 48877. Penrith: **Greystoke Gill Studio Pottery** Greystoke Gill 017684 83123, **Wetheriggs Pottery** Clifton Dykes 01768 892733.
LANCASHIRE: Fleetwood: **The Pottery Studio** (Autism Initiative) Farmer Parrs Animal World Rossall La 01253 772664. Oswaldtwistle: **The Naked Plate Ceramic Studio** Oswaldtwistle Mills 0161 866 9551.

SNOW SPORTS

CHESHIRE: Runcorn: **Ski Centre** Town Pk 01928 701965.
CUMBRIA: Carlisle: **Carlisle Ski Centre** Sark Cl 01228 561634. Kendal: **Kendal Ski Club** Canal Head North 01695 624199.
LANCASHIRE: Clitheroe: **Pendle Ski Club** Clitheroe Rd 01200 425222. Rawtenstall: **Ski Rossendale** Haslingden Old Rd 01706 226457.
MERSEYSIDE: Bebington: **The Oval Sports Centre** Old Chester Rd 0151 645 0596.

SPECTATOR SPORTS

Abbreviation: T: Tours.
CHESHIRE: Chester: **TCS Chester Jets Basketball Team** Northgate Arena Victoria Rd 0151 356 2616. Macclesfield: **Macclesfield Town FC** Moss Rose Ground London Rd 01625 264686. Tarporley: **Oulton Park Race Circuit** Little Budworth 01829 760301. Warrington: **Warrington Wolves** RLFC Halliwell Jones Stadium Winwick Rd 01925 248880.
CUMBRIA: Carlisle: **Carlisle United FC** Brunton Pk 01228 526237. Workington: **Workington Speedway** Derwent Pk Stadium 09066 555954.
GREATER MANCHESTER: Bolton: **Bolton Wanderers FC** Reebok Stadium Middlebrook Leisure and Retail Pk 01204 480601 T. Bury: **Bury FC** Gigg La 0161 764 4881. Manchester: **Belle Vue Aces Speedway** Kirkmanshulme La Gorton 0870 840 7550, **English Lacrosse Association** 26 Wood St 0161 834 4582, **Lancashire County Cricket Club** Warwick Rd Old Trafford 0161 282 4000, **Manchester City FC** City of Manchester Stadium Sports City 0161 231 3200 T, **Manchester Phoenix Ice Hockey Team** MEN Arena 0161 301 6851, **Manchester United FC** Sir Matt Busby Way Old Trafford 0870 442 1994 T, **National Cycling Centre** Manchester Velodrome Stuart St 0161 223 2244, **National Squash & Athletics Centre**

Rowsley St 0161 220 3800. Oldham: **Oldham Athletic FC** Boundary Pk 0161 624 4972, **Oldham Roughyeds RLFC** Waterloo St 0161 628 3677. Rochdale: **Rochdale FC** Willbutts La 01706 644648, **Rochdale Hornets RLFC** Sandy La 01706 648004. Salford: **Salford City Reds RLFC** The Willows Willows Rd 0161 736 6564. Stockport: **Sale Sharks RUFC** Edgeley Pk Hardcastle Rd 0161 286 8888, **Stockport County FC** Edgeley Pk Hardcastle Rd 0161 286 8888. Wigan: **Wigan Athletic FC** JJB Stadium Loire Dri 01942 774000, **Wigan Warriors RLFC** JJB Stadium Loire Dri 01942 774000.

LANCASHIRE: Blackburn: **Blackburn Rovers FC** Ewood Pk 0870 111 3232 T. Blackpool: **Blackpool FC** Seasiders Way 0870 443 1953. Burnley: **Burnley FC** 0870 443 1882. Carnforth: **Warton Stock Car Club** 01772 683100. Preston: **Preston North End FC** Deepdale 0870 442 1964.

MERSEYSIDE: Birkenhead: **Tranmere Rovers FC** Prenton Pk Prenton Rd West 0151 609 3333. Liverpool: **Everton FC** Goodison Pk 0151 330 2200 T, **Liverpool FC** Anfield Rd 0870 444 4949. St Helens: **St Helens RLFC** Dunriding La 0870 756 5252. Widnes: **Widnes Vikings RLFC** The Halton Stadium Lowerhouse La 0151 495 2250.

SPORTS & LEISURE CENTRES

* indicates centre has a swimming pool.

CHESHIRE: Alsager: **Alsager LC*** Hassall Rd 01270 875704. Bollington: **Bollington LC*** Heath Rd 01625 574774. Chester: **Northgate Arena*** Victoria Rd 01244 380444. Congleton: **Congleton LC*** Worrall St 01260 271552. Crewe: **Copenhall LC** Coronation St 01270 585698, **Shavington LC** Rope La 01270 663221. Ellesmere Port: **EPIC LC*** McGarva Way 0151 355 6432. Frodsham: **Frodsham LC** Queensway 01928 733953. Holmes Chapel: **Holmes Chapel LC** Selkirk Dri 01477 534401. Knutsford: **Knutsford LC*** Westfield Dri 01565 653321. Macclesfield: **Macclesfield LC*** Priory La Upton Priory 01625 615602. Middlewich: **Middlewich LC** St Anne's Walk 01606 832193. Northwich: **Moss Farm LCx** Winnington Rd Hartford 01606 783835, **Sir John Deane's LC*** Monarch Dri 01606 353930. Poynton: **Poynton LC*** Yew Tree La 01625 876442. Rudheath: **Rudheath LC** Shipbrook Rd 01606 41051. Runcorn: **Brookvale RC*** Barnfield Ave Murdishaw 01928 712051, **Halton SC** Murdishaw Ave Murdishaw 01928 714815. Sandbach: **Sandbach LC*** Middlewich Rd 01270 767129. Warrington: **Birchwood LC** Benson Rd 01925 458130, **Broomfields LC*** Broomfields Rd Stockton Heath 01925 268768, **Fordton LC*** Chiltern Rd Orford 01925 572504, **Great Sankey LC*** Barrowhall La 01925 724411, **Woolston LC*** Hall Rd 01925 813939. Widnes: **Kingsway LC*** Kingsway 0151 495 2200. Wilmslow: **Wilmslow LC*** Rectory Fields off Broadway 01625 533789. Winsford: **Winsford SCx*** The Drumber 01606 552776.

CUMBRIA: Barrow-in-Furness: **Park LC*** Greengate St 01229 871146. Cockermouth: **Cockermouth LC*** Castle Gate Dri 01900 823596. Dalton-in-Furness: **Dalton LC*** Chapel St 01229 463125. Grange-over-Sands: **Grange-over-Sands LC*** Berners Pk Rd 015395 38150. Kendal: **Kendal LC*** Burton Rd 01539 729777. Penrith: **Penrith LC*** Southend Rd 01768 863450. Ulverston: **Ulverston LC*** Priory Rd 01229 584110. Whitehaven: **Whitehaven SC** Flatt Walks 01946 695666. Workington: **Workington LC*** Newlands La South 01900 61771.

GREATER MANCHESTER: Altrincham: **Altrincham LC*** Oakfield Rd 0161 912 5900. Ashton-under-Lyne: **The Broadoak SC** off Broadoak Rd 0161 330 7975, **The Copley Centre*** Huddersfield Rd Stalybridge 0161 303 8118. Bolton: **Bolton Excel** Lower Bridgeman St 01204 334456, **Farnworth LC*** Brackley St Farnworth 01204 334477, **Harper Green Community LC** Harper Green Rd Farnworth 01204 334234, **Horwich LC*** Victoria Rd 01204 334488, **Ladybridge LC*** Junction Rd 01204 334432, **Little Lever Community LC** Church St 01204 334177, **Sharples Community LC*** Hillcot Rd Astley Bridge 01204 334224, **Turton Community LC*** Bromley Cross Rd 01204 334440, **Westhoughton Community LC*** Bolton Rd 01942 634810, **Withins Community LC** Newby Rd Breightmet 01204 334133. Bury: **Castle LC*** Bolton St 0161 253 6506. Droylsden: **Medlock LC*** Fold Ave 0161 370 3070. Eccles: **Fit City Eccles Centre*** Barton La 0161 787 7107. Manchester: **Abraham Moss LC*** Crescent Rd Crumpsall 0161 720 7622, **Belle Vue LC** Kirkmansulme La 0161 953 2470, **Broadway LC*** Broadway New Moston 0161 681 1060, **Chorlton LC*** Manchester Rd Chorlton-

cum-Hardy 0161 881 2130, **George H Carnell LC** Kingsway Pk Davyhulme 0161 912 2980, **Moss Side LC*** Moss La East 0161 226 5015, **National Squash & Athletics Centre** Rowsley St Eastlands 0161 220 3800, **Partington LC*** Chapel La 0161 912 5430, **Sale LC*** Broad Rd Sale 0161 912 3361, **Stretford LC*** Great Stone Rd 0161 912 4800, **Urmston LC*** Bowfell Rd Flixton 0161 912 2960, **Walton Park LC** Raglan Rd Sale 0161 912 3400, **Withington LC*** Burton Rd 0161 445 1046. Middleton: **Middleton LC*** Suffield St 0161 643 2894. Oldham: **Chadderton SC*** Middleton Rd 0161 911 3043, **Failsworth SC*** Brierley Ave 0161 911 5072, **Oldham SC*** Lord St 0161 911 4090, **Royton SC*** Park St 0161 911 3081. Rochdale: **Central LC*** Entwistle Rd 01706 639194, **Heywood SCx*** West Starkey St 01706 621040, **Littleborough Community SC** Calderbrook Rd 01706 756602, **Oulder Hill LCx*** Hudsons Walk Greave 01706 645522. Salford: **Fit City Broughton Centre** Camp St 0161 792 2375, **Fit City Cadishead Centre** Lords St 0161 775 7928, **Fit City Clarendon Centre*** Liverpool St 0161 736 1494, **Fit City Ordsall Centre** Trafford St 0161 848 0646, **Fit City Pendlebury*** Cromwell Rd 0161 793 1750. Stockport: **Avondale Leisure & Target Fitness Centre*** Heathbank Rd Cheadle Heath 0161 477 4242, **Cheadle Hulme RC** Woods La Cheadle Hulme 0161 485 4299, **Hazel Grove Pools & Target Fitness Centre*** Jacksons La 0161 439 5221, **Peel Moat Sports & Target Fitness Centre** Buckingham Rd Heaton Moor 0161 442 6416, **Ridge LC** Hibbert La Marple 0161 484 6688, **Romiley Pool & Target Fitness Centre** Holehouse Fold Romiley 0161 430 3437. Wigan: **Ashton LC*** Old Rd Ashton-in-Makerfield 01942 720826, **Hindley LC** Mornington Rd 01942 253142, **Howe Bridge SC*** Eckersley Fold La Atherton 01942 870403, **Robin Park Arena & SC** Loire Dri Newtown 01942 828550.
LANCASHIRE: Accrington: **Hyndburn SC** Henry St 01254 385945. Bacup: **Bacup Leisure Hall** Burnley Rd 01706 875550. Bamber Bridge: **Bamber Bridge LC*** Brindle Rd 01772 322012. Banks: **North Meols Community LC** Greaves Hall Ave 01704 212970. Blackburn: **Audley Sports & Community Centre** Chester St 01254 680012, **Shadsworth LC*** Shadsworth Rd 01254 264561. Blackpool: **Blackpool SC** West Pk Dri 01253 478470. Burnley: **Padiham LC*** Park Rd Padiham 01282 664588, **Palatine SC** St Annes Rd 01253 478484, **Thompson Centre*** Red Lion St 01282 664444. Burscough: **Burscough SC** Bobby Langton Way 01704 895266. Chorley: **All Seasons LC*** Water St 01257 515000. Clayton-le-woods: **Clayton Green SC** Clayton Green Rd 01257 515050. Clitheroe: **Roefield LC** Edisford Rd 01200 442188. Colne: **Pendle LC*** Crown Way 01282 661166. Darwen: **Darwen LC*** Green St 01254 771511. Fleetwood: **Fleetwood LC*** The Esplanade 01253 771505. Fullwood: **Fullwood LC*** Black Bull La 01772 716085. Garstang: **Garstang LC** Windsor Rd 01995 605410. Haslingden: **The Sports Centre** Helmshore Rd 01706 227016. Lancaster: **Lancaster University SC*** 01524 594000, **Salt Ayre SC*** Salt Ayre La 01524 847540. Leyland: **Leyland LC*** Lancastergate 01772 432285. Longridge: **Longridge SC** Preston Rd 01772 784474. Lostock Hall: **Lostock Hall SC** Todd La North 01772 628063. Penwortham: **Penwortham LC*** Crowshill Rd 01772 747272. Preston: **Preston Sports Arena** Tom Benson Way 01772 761000, **Westview LC*** Ribbleton La West View Ribbleton 01772 796788. Skelmersdale: **Skelmersdale SC** Digmoor Rd Digmoor 01695 723777. Thornton: **Thornton SC** Victoria Rd East 01253 824108.
MERSEYSIDE: Bebington: **The Oval*** Old Chester Rd 0151 645 0596. Birkenhead: **The Grange SC** Grange Rd West 0151 652 9336. Bootle: **Bootle LC*** Washington Pde 0151 330 3301, **Fernhill SC** Fernhill Rd 0151 933 7232. Crosby: **Crosby LC*** Mariners Rd 0151 932 9080. Garston: **Garston LC*** Long La 0151 233 5701. Halewood: **Halewood LC*** Baileys La 0151 443 2124. Huyton: **Huyton LC*** Roby Rd 0151 443 3786. Kirkby: **Kirkby SC** Valley Rd Westvale 0151 443 4404. Knowsley: **Heatwaves LC** Waterpark Dri 0151 443 2750. Leasowe: **Leasowe RC*** Twickenham Dri 0151 677 0916. Liverpool: **Cardinal Heenan SC*** Honeys Green La 0151 233 2345, **Croxteth SC** Altcross Rd 0151 548 3421, **Greenbank Sports Academy** Greenbank La 0151 280 7757, **Ellergreen LC*** Ellergreen Rd 0151 233 6295, **Park Road SC*** Steble St 0151 709 5395, **Toxteth Sport & LC** Upper Hill St 0151 709 7229. Newton-le-Willows: **Selwyn Jones SC*** Ashton Rd 01744 677970. Prescot: **Prescot LC** Warrington Rd 0151 430 7202, **Scotchbarn SC*** Scotchbarn La 0151 443 4643. St Helens: **Haydock LC** Clipsley La Haydock 01744 677505, **Queens Park LC*** Boundary Rd 01744 677465, **Sutton LC*** Elton Head Rd 01744 677375. Southport: **Dunes*** Esplanade 01704 537160. Thingwall: **Thingwall LC***

Thingwall Hall La 0151 220 7173. Walton: **Walton SC** Walton Hall Ave 0151 523 3472. West Kirby: **West Kirby Concourse** Grange Rd 0151 929 7801. Woodchurch: **Woodchurch LC*** Carr Bridge Rd 0151 677 9433.

SWIMMING POOLS (INDOOR)

Please also check the list of Sports and Leisure Centres above. Those marked with an * have a pool.
CHESHIRE: Chester: **Chester City Baths** Union St 01244 320898. Crewe: **Crewe Swimming Pool** Flag La 01270 560052. Nantwich: **Snowhill Swimming Pool** Wall La 01270 610606. Northwich: **Weaverham Pool** Russet Rd 01606 852705. Runcorn: **Runcorn Swimming Pool** Bridge St 01928 572114.
CUMBRIA: Appleby: **Appleby Swimming Pool** Chapel St 01768 351212. Carlisle: **Carlisle Swimming Pool** James St 01228 625777. Keswick: **Keswick Leisure Pool** The Old Station Station Rd 01768 772760. Whitehaven: **Copeland Pool** Cleator Moor Rd 01946 695021. Windermere: **Troutbeck Bridge Swimming Pool** 015394 43243.
GREATER MANCHESTER: Ashton-under-Lyne: **Ashton Pool** Water St 0161 330 1179, **Denton Pools** Victoria St 0161 336 1900, **Dukinfield Pool** Birch La 0161 330 5208, **Hyde Leisure Pool** Walker La 0161 368 4057. Bolton: **Jubilee Pool** Darley St 01204 334443. Manchester: **Levenshulme Pool** Barlow Rd 0161 224 4370, **Manchester Aquatics Centre** Oxford Rd 0161 275 9450, **Miles Platting Pool** Varley St 0161 205 8939. Oldham: **Crompton Pool** Farrow St Shaw 01706 844751, **Glodwick Pool** Nugget St 0161 911 3040. Radcliffe: **Radcliffe Pool** Green St 0161 253 7814. Rochdale: **Castleton Swimming Pool** Manchester Rd Castleton 01706 632117. Saddleworth: **Saddleworth Pool** Station Rd 01457 876668. Salford: **Fit City Broughton Pool** Great Cheetham St West 0161 792 2847, **Fit City Irlam Pool** Liverpool Rd 0161 775 4134, **Fit City Worsley Pool** Bridgewater Rd 0161 790 2084. Stockport: **Cheadle Pool** Shiers Dri Cheadle 0161 428 3216, **Grand Central Pools** Grand Central Sq Wellington Rd South 0161 474 7766, **Marple Swimming Pool** Stockport Rd Marple 0161 427 7070, **Reddish Vale Pool** Vale Road 0161 477 3544. Wigan: **Hindley Pool** Boarsdane Ave 01942 255401, **Tyldesley Pool** Castle St 01942 882722, **Wigan International Pool** Library St 01942 243345.
LANCASHIRE: Blackburn: **Daisyfield Pools** Daisy La 01254 277300. Blackpool: **Moor Park Swimming Pool** Bristol Ave 01253 478487, **Sandcastle Waterworld** South Promenade 01253 343602. Carnforth: **Carnforth Pool** Kellett Rd 01524 734699. Chorley: **Brinscall Swimming Baths** Lodge Bank Brinscall 01254 830453. Clitheroe: **Ribblesdale Pool** Edisford Rd 01200 424825. Garstang: **Garstang Swimming Centre** Oak Rd 01995 604340. Haslingden: **Haslingden Swimming Pool** East Bank Ave 01706 215883. Lancaster: **Hornby Swimming Pool** Melling Rd 015242 21119. Nelson: **Pendle Wavelengths** Leeds Rd 01282 661717. Ormskirk: **Park Pool** Park Rd 01695 576325. Poulton: **Swimming & Fitness Centre** Breck Rd 01253 891629. Preston: **Kirkham Baths** Station Rd 01772 682989. Ramsbottom: **Ramsbottom Pool** Porritt Way 01706 824208. St Anne's: **St Anne's Pool** The Island 01253 721325. Skelmersdale: **Nye Bevan Pool** Southway 01695 727111.
MERSEYSIDE: Birkenhead: **Europa Pools** Conway St 0151 647 4182. Kirkby: **Kirkby Pool** Hall La 0151 443 4303. Liverpool: **Deyes Lane Swimming Pool** Deyes La Maghull 0151 531 0933, **Newhall Swimming Pool** Longmoor La 0151 530 1218. St Helens: **Parr Swimming Pool** Ashcroft St 01744 677236. Seacombe: **Guinea Gap Baths** Riverview Rd 0151 639 9792. Woolton: **Woolton Swimmimg Pool** Quarry St 0151 428 1804.

SWIMMING POOLS (OUTDOOR)

CHESHIRE: Anderton(near): **Marbury Park Swimming Pool** Marbury Country Pk 07815 600364. Nantwich: **Nantwich Brine Pool** Wall La 01270 610606.
CUMBRIA: Penrith: **Askham Swimming Pool** 01931 712474, **Greystoke Swimming Pool** Church Rd 01768 483637, **Lazonby Swimming Pool** Barton Dale 01768 898346. Shap: **Shap Open Air Swimming Pool** Gayle Ave 01931 716572.

LANCASHIRE: Nelson: **Marsden Park Open Air Pool** Walton La 01282 661914.

THEATRES

CHESHIRE: Chester: **Gateway Theatre** Hamilton Pl 01244 340392. Crewe: **Lyceum Theatre** Heath St 01270 537333.
CUMBRIA: Cockermouth: **The Kirkgate Centre** Kirkgate 01900 826448. Keswick: **Theatre by the Lake** 017687 74411.
GREATER MANCHESTER: Altrincham: **Garrick Theatre** Barrington Rd 0161 928 1677. Ashton-under-Lyne: **Guide Bridge Theatre** Audenshaw Rd 0161 330 8078, **Tameside Hippodrome** Oldham Rd 0161 308 3223. Atherton: **Formby Hall** Alder St 01942 876496. Bolton: **The Albert Halls** Victoria Sq 01204 334433, **Octagon Theatre** Howell Croft South 01204 520661. Bury: **The Met** Market St 0161 761 2216. Manchester: **The Bridgewater Hall** Lower Mosley St 0161 907 9000, **Contact Theatre** Oxford Rd 0161 274 0600, **Dancehouse Theatre** Oxford Rd 0161 237 9753, **Opera House** Quay St 0870 401 9000, **Palace Theatre** Oxford St 0870 401 3000, **The Royal Exchange Theatre** St Ann's Sq 0161 833 9833. Oldham: **Coliseum Theatre** Fairbottom St 0161 624 2829. Rochdale: **Gracie Fields Theatre** Hudsons Walk 01706 645522. Romiley: **Forum** Compstall Rd 0161 430 6570. Saddleworth: **Millgate Theatre** Stonewood Rd 01457 874644. Sale: **Waterside Arts Centre** Northenden Rd 0161 912 5899. Salford: **The Lowry** Pier 8 Salford Quays 0161 876 2000, **Walk The Plank** (a moving theatre ship) 0161 736 8964. Wigan: **Little Theatre** Crompton St 01942 242561.
LANCASHIRE: Bacup: **Royal Court Theatre** Rochdale Rd 01706 874080. Blackpool: **Grand Theatre** 33 Church St 01253 290190, **Winter Gardens** Church St 01253 625252. Burnley: **Mechanics** Manchester Rd 01282 664400. Chorley: **Chorley Little Theatre** Dole La 01257 275123. Darwen: **Darwen Library Theatre** Knott St 01254 706006. Lancaster: **The Dukes** Moor La 01524 598500, **Grand Theatre** Saint Leonardsgate 01524 64695. Lytham: **Lowther Pavilion** West Beach 01253 735211. Preston: **Guild Hall Theatre** Lancaster Rd 01772 258858, **Playhouse** Market St West 01772 252288.
MERSEYSIDE: Birkenhead: **Little Theatre** Grange Rd West 0151 647 6593. Liverpool: **Empire Theatre** Lime St 0870 606 3536, **Everyman Theatre** Hope St 0151 709 4776, **Neptune Theatre** Hanover St 0151 709 7844, **Olympia** West Derby Rd 0151 263 6633, **Philharmonic Hall** Hope St 0151 709 3789, **Playhouse** Williamson Sq 0151 709 4776, **Royal Court Theatre** Roe St 0151 709 4321, **Unity Theatre** Hope Pl 0151 709 4988. New Brighton: **Floral Pavilion Theatre** Virginia Rd 0151 639 4360. St Helens: **Theatre Royal** Corporation St 01744 756000. Southport: **Little Theatre** Hoghton St 01704 530521, **Theatre and Floral Hall** The Promenade 0870 607 7560. Wirral: **Gladstone Theatre** Greendale Rd Port Sunlight 0151 643 8757.

WATERSPORTS

Also check out 'Outdoor Pursuits' as many companies offer watersports alongside land-based activities. For abbreviations see key at the beginning of this chapter.
CHESHIRE: Frodsham: **Sail Sports** Manley Mere 01928 740243 C S W.
CUMBRIA: Keswick: **Derwentwater Marina** Portinscale 017687 72912 C K Rt S TB W, **Nichol End Marine** Portinscale 017687 73082 C K M Ro SD W. Windermere: **Low Wood Watersports Centre** Ambleside Rd Low Wood 015394 39441 K M S WS, **Windermere Outdoor Adventure** Rayrigg Rd 015394 47183 C K S W.
GREATER MANCHESTER: Littleborough: **Hollingworth Lake Water Activity Centre** Lake Bank 01706 370499 K S W. Rochdale: **Whitworth Waterski & Recreation Centre** Cowm Reservoir Tong La 01760 852534 Wb WS. Salford: **Salford Watersports Centre** 15 The Quays 0161 877 7252 C K S W. Trafford: **Trafford Watersports Centre** Sale Water Pk 0161 962 0118 B C K Rt S.
MERSEYSIDE: Liverpool: **Merseysport** 110 Mariners Wharf Queens Dock 0151 708 9322 C PB S W. Wirral: **Wirral Sailing Centre** West Kirby Marine Lake South Pde 0151 625 3292 K S W.

Learn first aid skills your way

Learning first aid is easy. It only takes a few minutes to learn the basic skills that could make a crucial difference should the children in your care be involved in an accident. There's no limit to the ways you can learn first aid. If you're interested in courses, we offer a wide selection – ranging from two to 28 hours – all across the UK. And if you're part of a group – for example parents, post-natal, Brownies or Cubs – we can even come to you.

Call your local Red Cross branch or 0870 170 9222 to find out more.

You can also learn at home. The Red Cross offers an exciting range of first aid products that ensure you can learn what you want, when you want.

First Aid for Children – Fast (£9.99)
This is an indispensable reference guide for dealing quickly and confidently with any childhood emergency, from cuts and grazes to choking and poisoning.

Save a Life DVD/VHS (£9.99)
A quick and easy guide to learning the vital first aid skills that could help you save a life. Available on DVD or VHS.

First aid kit for child carers (£15.20)
A specially produced kit for parents and all those who care for children.

5-minute first aid books (£6.99)
Our 5-minute guides offer a radical new way of learning first aid. These self-study books are full of bite-sized sections, each demonstrating a first aid skill in basic, jargon-free language.

5-minute first aid for children
5-minute first aid for babies

For more information, visit redcross.org.uk/firstaidproducts or, to order our products, call

0870 170 9222

BritishRedCross

Someone should help

Someone should call 999

Someone will know what to do

I'm someone

Someone will make sure he's ok

Thousands of children are killed or seriously injured on our roads each year

Many of these tragic deaths could be prevented if immediate first aid was given at the scene.

Everyone – regardless of age or ability – should have some first aid skills. Children, particularly those moving from primary to secondary schools, face an increased risk on their daily journey. And should something go wrong, just a little first aid knowledge can make a big difference.

Unfortunately, recent research shows that more than half of children in the UK would not know what to do. That's why the British Red Cross, in partnership with Toyota, is encouraging young people and their parents to find out about road safety and learn first aid skills. All it takes is a few minutes – and you could have a life-saving impact

What to do if you see a road accident
1. Stop! You can help.
2. Stay safe and keep calm.
3. Keep the casualty breathing.
4. Stop the bleeding.
5. Call 999.

For an exciting range of first aid video clips, games, tips and advice for parents, visit redcross.org.uk/roadsafety

"As a major vehicle manufacturer, Toyota bears a particular responsibility toward road safety. Toyota's ultimate goal is to reduce road traffic accidents, deaths and injuries to zero" Piet Steel, Vice-President, External Affairs, Toyota Motor Europe
yota.co.uk/roadsafety

In partnership with **TOYOTA**

27

Fun *without* WaspBane

When wasps have fun, it's often at our expense! Compared with other leading wasp traps, WaspBane has been shown to reduce sting rates in visitor attractions by as much as 97%*.
Pesticide free, clean and easy to use WaspBane is probably the safest wasp trap in the world.

WaspBane; helping to make your environment safer!

For more information visit
www.waspbane.com
or call 01480 414644

*When used as part of a comprehensive wasp control strategy

WaspBane
EFFECTIVE ELIMINATION™

Cheshire

With soft rolling plains and pretty market towns, Cheshire has a wide variety of attractions with many entries in the 'Farms' and 'History' sections reflecting its traditional heritage. Chester leads the way with stunning architecture, family museums, activities and thousands of years of history.

ADVENTURE, FUN & SOFT PLAY

Chester, Funky Monkey's Playhouse, *Grange Road, www.monkeytown.co.uk 01244 377229.*
By day the soft play equipment entertains younger children and in the evenings the older ones run free for a game of laser tag. Open daily, 10am-9.30pm. Groups Birthdays **Refreshments Open all year** Price A.
KK5, *Marley Way, Central Trading Estate, Saltney, 01244 677357.*
Enjoy slides, rope bridges and ball ponds, or will you get lost in the maze? Open daily, 10am-7pm. Groups Birthdays **Refreshments Open all year** Price A.
Quasar, *Volunteer Street, 01244 400500.*
Enjoy indoor sci-fi adventure games with sound and special effects. Open daily, 11am-9pm. Groups Birthdays **Open all year** Price P.

Crewe, Funsters, *Stalbridge Road, 01270 500525.*
An indoor play centre with slides, ball pools and dressing-up clothes. Also GT racing slot-car circuit to hire by prior booking (www.gtracing.co.uk). Open daily from 10am, closing times vary. Groups Birthdays **Refreshments Open all year** Price A.

Frodsham, Adventure Trail, *Manley Mere, www.sail-sports.co.uk 01928 740243.*
Prepare to get wet and muddy. Rope swings and monkey climbs help you to traverse the river for a real adventure. Open daily, Apr-Oct, 10am-6pm; winter, Sat-Sun & school hols, 10am-5pm. Groups **Refreshments Open all year** Price B.
Cocos Play Barn, *Lady Heyes Craft & Antique Centre, Kingsley Road, 01928 789028.*
A large and exciting three-storey soft play area for all ages, with a separate enclosed court for football and basketball. Major additions are planned for 2006. Open daily, times vary. Groups Birthdays **Refreshments Open all year** Price A.

Nantwich, Reaseheath Maize Maze, *www.reaseheath.ac.uk 01270 613215.*
They've had Pirates, Dinosaurs and Sea Creatures. What do you think this year's theme will be? Open daily, late Jul-early Sept, 11am-6pm (allow enough time to get out!). Groups **Price B.**

Neston, Jumpin' Jack's House, *High Street, www.jumpinjackshouse.co.uk 0151 353 8833.*
A good mix of slides, climbing equipment and ball pools to entertain children. Open Mon-Sat, 9.30am-6.30pm, Sun, 11am-4pm. Groups Birthdays **Refreshments Open all year** Price A.

Northwich, Joe Crow's Play Stacks, *Blakemere Craft Centre, Chester Road, www.playstacks.co.uk 01606 301321.*
Explore the soft play area with separate section for under 5s and then visit the computer games 'Zapper Zone'. New party plan and seating area for 2006. Groups Birthdays **Refreshments Open all year** Price A.

Stretton(near), The Amazing Maize Maze, *between Appleton Thorn and Stretton, www.naturaladventures.co.uk 01925 268495.*
Enjoy this giant puzzle with mini mazes, power carts, tipi building, events throughout the season and visitor centre. Open daily, mid Jul-early Sept, 10am-6pm, weekends only in Sept. Groups Birthdays **Price B.**

Warrington, Giggles Playmill, *Evans House, Norman Street, www.gigglesplaymill.com 01925 445753.*
Newly improved and over 700 square metres. There are separate play areas for children and toddlers, a bouncy castle, a sports court, climbing wall and ball blasters. Open daily, 9.30am-7.30pm. Groups Birthdays **Refreshments Open all year Price A.**

Gulliver's World, *www.gulliversfun.co.uk 01925 444888.*
Thrilling rides designed for children between the ages of 2 and 13. From modern rollercoasters to pedal cars and scooters, there is something for every child. Telephone for opening times and prices. Groups Birthdays **Refreshments Price D.**

Jungle Gym Play & Party, *Chetham Court, Winwick Quay, www.thejunglegym.co.uk 01925 659995.*
Swing, slide, climb and scramble like a real explorer. Three-storey fun with separate Mini Cubs area. Children can enter from ground level or from the mezzanine lounge. Open daily, 10am-6pm. Groups Birthdays Refreshments Open all year Price A.

Waverton, Crocky Trail, *Guy Lane, www.crockytrail.co.uk 01244 335753.*
A mile-long adventure trail, with a vertical roundabout! Can you stay on The Spinning Wheel or the Titanic slide? Escape the Spider Trap and see how long you can be `King of the Castle'. Open weekends and school hols, 10am-5pm. Groups **Open all year Price B.**

Winsford, Jolly Jesters, *Knights Grange Sports Complex, Grange Lane, www.jestersplaybarn.co.uk 01606 869573.*
Hold court at this castle-themed playbarn decorated with pictures of knights and court jesters. Slides, ball ponds, tunnels and separate toddler and craft areas. Open daily, 10am-6pm. Groups Birthdays **Refreshments Open all year Price A.**

FARMS, WILDLIFE & NATURE PARKS

Chester, Chester Zoo, *Upton-by-Chester, www.chesterzoo.org 01244 380280.*
With over 7000 animals in 110 acres of award-winning gardens, you really need a full day to explore and see the amazing range of wildlife. There is always something new to see and do, explore the 'Spirit of the Jaguar' enclosure and the 'Twilight Zone'. Take a trip on the Zoofari railway or the seasonal water bus boat. Daily programme of activities and events include feeding time, and the Fun Ark outdoor play area is a great way to let off some steam. Open daily from 10am (except Christmas and Boxing Day). Please call or visit the website for closing times and prices. Schools Birthdays **Refreshments Open all year Check out page 36.**

Crewe(near), Lakemore Farm Park, *Clay Lane, Haslington, 01270 253556.*
A beautiful farm park which is home to llamas, pigs and pigmy goats. There are indoor and outdoor play areas, crazy golf and craft sessions during school holidays. Open Easter-Oct, Wed-Sun, 10am-5pm, and daily during school hols. Schools Birthdays **Price A.**

Ellesmere Port, Blue Planet Aquarium, *Cheshire Oaks, www.blueplanetaquarium.com 0151 357 8804.*
Travel underwater via the moving tunnel to watch the sharks feed, or tickle the rays in the rock pool. Afterwards, sail away on the Octopus Adventure playground. Open daily from 10am, closing times vary. Schools Birthdays **Refreshments Open all year Price D.**

Knutsford, Gauntlet Bird of Prey, Eagle and Vulture Park, *next to Fryers Roses, Manchester Road, www.gauntlet.info 01565 754419.*
Regular flying displays with hands-on demonstrations and falconry courses. There are over 80 birds of prey at the centre. Watch out for photography days in 2006. Open daily, Mar-Oct, 11am-5pm, Nov-Feb, Sat-Sun, 11am-4pm. Schools Birthdays **Open all year Price A.**

Malpas, Cholmondeley Castle Garden, *01829 720383.*

Stroll through the magnificent gardens and then see rare breed farm animals in the paddock. Children's Corner with small animals and free-flying birds in the aviary (Castle is not open to the public). Special events, lakeside picnic area and two play areas. Open Apr-Sept, Wed-Thurs, Sun and Bank Hols, 11.30am-5pm. Groups Refreshments Price B.

Nantwich, The Palms Tropical Oasis, *Stapeley Water Gardens, London Road, Stapely,* *www.stapeleywg.com 0845 3445684.*

Talk to the toucans in the tropical house, home to many small mammals, birds, reptiles and fish. See the giant Amazon Water Lily or find tranquillity in the Italian garden. Open Mon-Sat, 9am-6pm (5pm mid Sept-mid Mar), Sun, 10am-4pm. Schools Birthdays Refreshments Open all year Price B Check out page 32.

Northwich, Cheshire Waterlife Aquatic and Falconry Centre, *Blakemere Craft Centre,* *Sandiway, www.cheshire-waterlife.co.uk 01606 882223.*

Find aviaries housing several birds of prey and frequent flying displays. Aviaries open daily, 10am-5pm. Flying displays Mar-Sept, telephone for times. Schools Birthdays Open all year Price A.

Northwich(near), Stockley Farm, *Arley, www.stockleyfarm.co.uk 01565 777323.*

Begin with a tractor ride to this organic dairy farm. Visit the cattle and smaller animals and then feed the lambs. Soft play, an adventure playground, pottery and birds of prey make an eclectic mix of fun. Open Mar-early Oct, Sat-Sun and Bank Hols, 11am-5pm (Tues-Sun during school hols). Schools Birthdays Refreshments Price B.

Tarporley, Cotebrook Shire Horse Centre and Countryside Park, *Cotebrook,* *www.cotebrookshirehorses.co.uk 01829 760506.*

A small, friendly working stud with helpful staff who introduce the animals and horses. Nature trail and picnic area. Ideal for horse-lovers. Open daily, 10am-5pm. Schools Open all year Price B.

FREE PLACES

Buwardsley, Cheshire Workshops, *01829 770401.*

See candles made and glass artists at work. There are many activities for children at weekends and in school holidays, including candle dipping and the penny arcade (telephone to book). Outdoor play area. Open daily, 10am-5pm. Groups Birthdays Refreshments Open all year Price P.

Chester is the most complete walled city in Britain and famous for its magnificent half-timbered buildings and Roman connections. The city centre is a vibrant mix of shops, cafés and stunning architecture including The Rows, with two tiered shopping galleries and medieval walkways. Why not follow the Millennium Trail, a city walk covering buildings from the last 2,000 years, or simply walk around the city walls? For details contact Chester Visitor Centre.

Chester Visitor Centre, *Vicar's Lane, www.chestertourism.com 01244 402111.*

Trace your family name or discover 2,000 years of history at the Roman Amphitheatre exhibition. Open Mon-Sat, 10am-5pm, Sun, 10am-4pm. Schools Open all year.

Grosvenor Museum, *27 Grosvenor Street, www.chestercc.gov.uk 01244 402008.*

Follow video tours with a keeper as a guide and discover the computerised collections in the gallery. Find out about Deva, the military fortress. Open Mon-Sat, 10.30am-5pm, Sun, 1-4pm. Schools Open all year.

Grosvenor Park, *Vickers Lane, close to the town centre.*

Wander through one of the finest examples of a Victorian park. A miniature railway runs daily in school holidays and at weekends, 10am-6pm. Groups Open all year.

Chester(near), Cheshire Farm Ice Cream, *Drumlan Hall Farm, Newton Lane, Tattenall,*
01829 770446.
A working dairy farm with a selection of animals and aviaries for rescued birds of prey. Playbarn, playground and a wonderful selection of ice creams and sorbets. Open daily, Apr-Oct, 10am-5.30pm, Nov-Mar, 10.30am-5pm. (Closed for two weeks, early Jan.) Schools Birthdays Refreshments **Open all year.**

Crewe, Queens Park, *Wistaston Road.*
Listen to music from the bandstand on Sundays in summer in this traditional park with large boating lake and pets corner. **Open all year.**

Englesea Brook, Englesea Brook Chapel and Museum, *01270 820836.*
Experience a Victorian Sunday school where children can enjoy role-play. Explore the Chapel, graveyard and museum and play with Victorian toys. Open Apr-Nov, Thurs-Sat & Bank Hol Mons, 10.30am-5.15pm, Sun, 1.30-5.15pm. Schools.

Great Budworth, Great Budworth Real Dairy Ice Cream Farm, *Heath Lane,*
www.icecreamfarm.co.uk 01606 891211.
A family-run dairy farm with many regular flavours of home-made ice cream plus seasonal variations. A maze trail in August and other events throughout summer. Open daily, Apr-Oct, 12noon-6pm, Mar and Nov-Dec, Sat-Sun, 1-5pm. Schools **Refreshments.**

Macclesfield, West Park Museum, *Prestbury Road, www.macclesfield.silk.museum 01625 619831.*
Located in one of the earliest public parks, the museum is home to a permanent Egyptian collection which includes a mummy case and afterlife displays. Activity sheets, temporary exhibits and special events. Open Easter-Oct, Tues-Sat, 1.30-4.30pm, Nov-Easter, 1-4pm. Schools **Open all year.**

Macclesfield(near), Blaze Farm, *on A54 Congleton to Buxton road, www.blazefarm.com*
01260 227229.
Find delicious home-made ice cream. Watch the cows being milked and lambing in spring. There is pottery painting and a wildlife trail. Open daily, 10am-5pm. Schools Birthdays **Refreshments Open all year.**

Nantwich, Nantwich Museum, *Pillory Street, www.nantwichmuseum.org.uk 01270 627104.*
Learn the history of the market town. Discover Nantwich's part in the Civil War. Children's competitions during school holidays. Open Apr-Sept, Mon-Sat, 10.30am-4.30pm, Oct-Mar, Tues-Sat. Schools **Open all year.**

Northwich(near), Delamere Forest Park, *Delamere, 01606 889792.*
Take a picnic and explore the countryside. Visitor centre and ranger-led organised activities throughout the year, with extra events during school holidays. Schools **Refreshments Open all year.**

Runcorn, Town Park, *Palacefields.*
Landscaped gardens and a miniature railway taking you on a mile-long journey. Railway operates most Suns, 1.30-4.30pm. **Open all year.**

Warrington, Walton Hall Gardens, *Walton Lea Road, Higher Walton, 01925 601617.*
An undulating park with small zoo, great play area, crazy golf and pitch and putt. Heritage Centre and ranger service with special events and activities. Park open daily until dusk (zoo closes earlier). Schools **Refreshments Open all year.**
Warrington Museum and Art Gallery, *Museum Street, www.warrington.gov.uk 01925 442392.*
Visit the 'time tunnel', try on a costume and guess what's in the 'feely' boxes. Have a go at fossil rubbing or make a dinosaur flip book. Changing exhibitions. Open Mon-Fri, 9am-5pm, Sat, 9am-4pm. Schools **Open all year.**

Alderley Edge, Nether Alderley Mill, NT, *Congleton Road, 01625 584412.*
Explore this old water mill set beside a tranquil millpond with its Victorian machinery. Regular flour grinding demonstrations. Open Apr-Oct, Thurs, 1-5pm, Sun and Bank Hol Mons, 11am-5pm. Schools **Price A.**

Arley, Arley Hall & Gardens, *www.arleyhallandgardens.com 01565 777353.*
The historic house and gardens have a regular calendar of children's events, including theatre presentations, Easter with Beatrix Potter, a Wizard Week and a Halloween Festival. Gardens open Apr-Oct, Tues-Sun, 11am-5pm, winter, Sat-Sun. House open Apr-Oct, Tues, Sun & Bank Hols, 12noon-5pm. Groups **Refreshments Open all year Price B.**

Bunbury, Bunbury Watermill, *Mill Lane, 01829 261422.*
Witness the power of water as it turns machinery used to grind grain into flour in this restored Victorian water mill. Guided tours by prior arrangement at any time all year round. Public opening Apr-Sept, Sun, 1.30-4.30pm. Schools Birthdays **Price A.**

Chester, Cheshire Military Museum, *The Castle, www.chester.ac.uk 01244 327617.*
Use computers and hands-on exhibits to guide yourself through the military history of Cheshire. Events and activities. Open daily, 10am-4pm. Schools **Open all year Price A.**

Dewa Roman Experience, *Pierpoint Lane, Bridge Street, www.dewaromanexperience.co.uk 01244 343407.*
Spend time in the hands-on studio and visit the reconstructed street to experience the smells and sounds of a Roman fortress. Open Feb-Nov, Mon-Sat, 9am-5pm, Sun, 10am-5pm; Dec-Jan, daily, 10am-4pm. Schools Birthdays **Open all year Price B.**

Guided Tours, *01244 402445.*
Try the Roman Soldier Wall Patrol (during school holidays) or the Ghost Tour which runs all year round. Unlock the secrets of Chester on the Secret Chester Tour (May-Oct, 2hrs). Contact the Tourist Information Centre for more details.

Many Museums have FREE entry. Check out the Free Places section.

Congleton, Congleton Museum, *Market Square, www.congletonmuseum.co.uk 01260 276360.*
The emphasis is on local history here. Follow the time line and use touch-screen computers to discover more. Activities during school holidays. Open Tues-Fri & Sun, 12noon-4.30pm, Sat, 10am-4.30pm. Schools **Open all year Price A.**

Little Moreton Hall, NT, *01260 272018.*
Learn about life in Tudor times by taking a guided tour. The events programme includes 'living history' weekends and family activities. Open 25th Mar–5th Nov, Wed-Sun, 11.30am-5pm; 11th Nov-17th Dec, Sat-Sun, 11.30am-4pm. Schools **Refreshments Price B.**

Crewe, The Railway Age, *Vernon Way, www.therailwayage.co.uk 01270 212130.*
An interesting collection ranging from steam trains to modern advanced passenger trains. Pull levers in the signal box or have a game of giant noughts and crosses. Open Sat-Sun, Easter-Sept, 10am-4pm. Schools Birthdays **Price B.**

Ellesmere Port, The Boat Museum, *South Pier Road, www.boatmuseum.org.uk 0151 355 5017.*
Canals in their heyday. Board a narrowboat or visit the lock-keepers' cottages. Imagine life before railways arrived. New exhibitions are planned for 2006. Children's activities and events. Open daily, Apr-Oct, 10am-5pm, Nov-Mar, Sat-Wed, 11am-4pm. Schools Birthdays **Refreshments Open all year Price B.**

Farndon(near), Stretton Watermill, *on A534 to Broxton, www.strettonwatermill.org.uk 01606 41331.*
Situated in lovely countryside, this small working water mill has displays and a picnic area. Open Apr & Sept, Sat-Sun, 1-5pm; May-Aug, Tues-Sun, 1-5pm. Schools **Price A.**

Knutsford, Tabley House, *www.tableyhouse.co.uk 01565 750151.*
This richly furnished Palladian house has a children's activity booklet, parklands and picnic area. Open Apr-end Oct, Thurs-Sun & Bank Hol Mons, 2-5pm. Schools **Price B.**
Tatton Park, *www.tattonpark.org.uk 01625 534400.*
An historic country estate. Feed the animals in the rare breeds farm or tackle the quiz around the mansion. The gardens, parkland and excellent adventure playground are great for burning energy. Special events and activities. Opening times vary. Schools **Refreshments Open all year Price B.**

Macclesfield, Jodrell Bank Visitor Centre and Arboretum, *www.jb.man.ac.uk 01477 571339.*
Exceptional views of the telescope make children curious about the exhibition. Picnic area, playground, nature and planet trails, special events and activities. Open daily, mid Mar-Oct, 10.30am-5.30pm, Nov-mid Mar, Tues-Fri, 10.30am-3pm, Sat-Sun, 11am-4pm. Schools **Refreshments Open all year Price A.**
Macclesfield Silk Museums, *Roe Street, www.macclesfield.silk.museum 01625 613210.*
Three museums within easy walking distance of each other chart the progress of silk, from China to design and use in period and modern costumes. See restored handlooms in operation and experience life at the turn of the century. Open Mon-Sat, 11am-5pm, Sun, 12noon-4pm. Schools **Refreshments Open all year Price B.**

Mouldsworth, Mouldsworth Motor Museum, *Smithy Lane, www.mouldsworthmotormuseum.com 01928 731781.*
An interesting collection of cars, cycles, pedal cars and associated memorabilia in a stunning Art-Deco setting. Free children's quiz sheet with prizes. Open Feb-Nov, 12noon-5pm, Suns & Bank Hols; Weds during Jul & Aug. Schools Birthdays **Price A.**

Nantwich, Hack Green Secret Nuclear Bunker, *www.hackgreen.co.uk 01270 629219.*
Explore displays and re-created scenes in this former nuclear bunker. Send a Morse code message or try out a Home Office bed! Soviet Spy Mouse Trail for younger children. Open daily, Apr-Oct, 10.30am-5.30pm, Nov & Jan-Mar, Sat-Sun, 11am-4.30pm. Schools **Refreshments Price B.**

Northwich, Anderton Boat Lift, *Lift Lane, Anderton, www.andertonboatlift.co.uk 01606 786777.*
The world's first boat lift. Restoration work is complete and there is an operations centre with exhibition area and interactive activities. Boat and lift trips are available at extra charge. Open daily, Easter-Oct, 10am-5pm. Schools Birthdays **Refreshments Price A.**
The Salt Museum, *162 London Road, www.saltmuseum.org.uk 01606 41331.*
Follow the story of salt and the industry which has grown around it. Interactive gallery, free quiz sheets, exhibitions and special events. Open Tues-Fri, 10am-5pm, Sat-Sun, 2-5pm; also Bank Hol Mons and every Mon in Aug. Schools Birthdays **Open all year Price A.**

Runcorn, Norton Priory Museum & Gardens, *Tudor Road, Manor Park, www.nortonpriory.org 01928 569895.*
A family-friendly historic site with sculpture trail and displays of real objects depicting life in the monastery. Open Apr-Oct, Mon-Fri, 12noon-5pm, Sat-Sun, 12noon-6pm; Nov-Mar, daily, 12noon-4pm. Schools **Refreshments Open all year Price B.**

Styal, Quarry Bank Mill & Styal Estate, NT, *01625 527468.*
Unearth the story of cotton at a working mill where fabric is still produced. See the enormous waterwheel and Apprentice House. Interactive exhibits and school holiday activities. Mill open daily, mid Mar-Sept, 11am-5pm, Oct-mid Mar, Wed-Sun, 11am-4pm. Check for Apprentice House. Schools **Refreshments Open all year Price B.**

Tarporley(near), Beeston Castle, EH, *01829 260464.*
Imagine life as a soldier in this medieval fortress, set high above the Cheshire plains. Special events throughout the year. Open daily, Apr-Sept, 10am-6pm, Oct-Mar, 10am-4pm. Schools **Open all year** Price A.

Widnes, Catalyst – Science Discovery Centre, *Mersey Road, www.catalyst.org.uk 0151 420 1121.*
Hands-on activities and touch-screen computers guide you through the world of science and the use of chemicals in everyday objects. Workshops during school holidays. Open Tues-Fri and Bank Hol Mons, 10am-5pm, Sat-Sun, 11am-5pm, & most Mons in school hols. Schools Birthdays Refreshments **Open all year** Price B **Check out advert below.**

TRIPS & TRANSPORT

BOAT TRIPS

Chester, Bithell Boats, *Boating Station, Souters Lane, www.showboatsofchester.co.uk 01244 325394.*
Regular 30-minute cruises on the River Dee and a two-hour cruise to Ironbridge. Private charter also. Operates daily, summer, 11am-5.30pm; winter, Sat-Sun, 11am-4pm. Schools Birthdays **Open all year**.

BUS TRIPS

Chester, City Sightseeing, *www.city-sightseeing.com 0871 666 0000.*
Hop on board an open-top bus for a tour of the city's attractions with running commentary and Kids Club activity pack. Operates Mar-Oct. **Price B.**

Cumbria

Cumbria is home to The Lake District National Park and has breathtaking scenery of enormous proportions. Scafell Pike is the highest mountain in England, whilst Windermere is the largest natural lake. This landscape makes Cumbria and the Lake District the ideal place for watersports and outdoor activities, so check out the 'Sports & Leisure' chapter for more details. If you enjoy a more relaxed pace, there are plenty of museums showing the industrial and cultural heritage of the area, from mining and cottage industries to the Roman influence of Emperor Hadrian. Don't forget the coastline with its fishing heritage and varied wildfowl.

ADVENTURE, FUN & SOFT PLAY

Ambleside, Bonkers and Bobbies Den, *Piano Café, 5 Market Cross, 015394 31198.*
Relax with a drink while the children have fun on the slides and in the ball pool. Open daily, 10am-4pm. Groups Birthdays **Refreshments Open all year Price A.**

Barrow-in-Furness, LazerZone, *The Custom House, 1 Abbey Road, www.funshineindoors.co.uk 01229 823823.*
Advanced laser tag interactive arena where you can zap your friends and enemies! Open Mon-Fri, 3-8pm, Sat-Sun & Bank Hols, 10am-8pm. Groups Birthdays **Open all year Price P.**
PlayZone, *The Custom House, 1 Abbey Road, www.funshineindoors.co.uk 01229 823823.*
Three tiers of fun in this underwater-themed soft play area. Slides, ropes, ball pools and much more. Open daily, 9.30am-6pm. Groups Birthdays **Refreshments Open all year Price A.**

Carlisle, Laser Quest, *Bush Bow, Victoria Viaduct, www.lquk.com 01228 511155.*
A sci-fi, space-age game of tag with laser guns. Open Mon-Fri, 11am-9pm, Sat, 10am-9pm, Sun, 10am-7pm. Groups Birthdays **Open all year Price P.**
Funtazia, *Currock Road Trade Centre, 01228 409408.*
An exciting play structure on three levels with 'Little Tykes Den' for toddlers. Opening times vary. Groups Birthdays **Open all year Price P.**
Magic Castle Adventure Playground, *Atlas Works, Nelson Street, 01228 401095.*
Two levels of fun with separate under 5s area. Bouncy castle, slides, tunnels and rope bridges entertain older children. Open Mon-Fri, 10am-5pm, Sat-Sun, 10am-3.30pm. Groups Birthdays **Open all year Price P.**

Grange-over-Sands, Lakeland Miniature Village, *Winder Lane, Flookburgh, www.lakelandminiaturevillage.com 015395 58500.*
Enjoy the Lakeland landscape in miniature, made from local slate. There is a play area and a new Japanese tea house is planned for 2006. Open daily, 10.30am-dusk. Groups **Open all year Price A.**

Grizedale, Go Ape! *High Wire Forest Adventure, Grizedale Forest Visitor Centre, www.goape.co.uk 0870 444 5562.*
This extreme outdoor adventure course has rope bridges, Tarzan swings and zip slides. Wear suitable clothing. Advance booking essential, age and height restrictions apply, and adult supervision required. Open daily, Feb half term and Apr-Oct; Nov & Mar, Sat-Sun only. Groups Birthdays **Price G.**

Kendal, Fun for Kids, *Parkside Road, 01539 735556.*
A soft play area with a variety of equipment including a bouncy castle. Open Mon-Sat, 9.30am-6pm, Sun, 10am-6pm. Groups Birthdays **Refreshments Open all year Price A.**

Kendal(near), Lakeland Maize Maze, *Raines Hall Farm, Sedgewick, www.lakelandmaze.co.uk*
015395 61760.
A nine-acre maze with accompanying quiz trail. If you get out, there are small mazes, table-top
puzzles, space hoppers, sand pit, play area and more. Open daily, mid Jul-Sept, 10am-6pm, check
dates before visiting. Groups **Price B.**

Maryport, Clown-A-Round, *Station Street, 01900 818811.*
Coco's Corner for under 3s and climbing frames, ball pools, tunnels and slides for older children.
This adventure play centre also has creche facilities. Open Mon-Sat, 10am-4pm. Groups
Birthdays **Refreshments Open all year Price A.**

Milnthorpe, Fire Fighter Experience, *around J36 of M6, www.firefighterexperience.com*
015395 64242.
Put on the safety clothing, ride the fire engine and extinguish real fires under the supervision of
experienced Fire Fighters. By appointment only. Prices vary with packages. Schools Birthdays
Open all year.

Penrith, Noah's Ark Soft Play Centre, *Burrowgate, 01768 890640.*
A bouncy castle, ball pools and slides to use up all that surplus energy! Open 10am-3.45pm
during term time. Groups Birthdays **Refreshments Open all year Price A.**

Silloth-on-Solway, The Sunset Leisure Centre, *Stanwix Park Holiday Centre, www.stanwix.com*
016973 32666.
A day pass gets access to the Leisure Centre, swimming pools and soft play area. Bowling and
amusements also available. Pass includes evening entertainment. Open daily, 9am-9pm. Groups
Birthdays **Open all year Price C.**

Whitehaven, Billy Bears Fun Centre, *Haig Enterprise Park, Kells, 01946 690003.*
A play area specifically for the under 6s with bouncy castle, climbing frame, cars and bikes. Open
Mon-Fri, 10am-3pm, Sat-Sun, 10am-1pm. Groups Birthdays **Open all year Price A.**

Workington, Funky Monkeys Fun Factory, *Derwent Howe Industrial Estate, Peart Road,*
01900 64222.
Let off steam in this indoor adventure play centre. Special area for under 4s. Open Tues-Sun,
10am-4pm. Groups Birthdays **Open all year Price P.**

FARMS, WILDLIFE & NATURE PARKS

Carlisle, Highhead Sculpture Valley, *Highhead Farm, Ivegill, www.highheadsculpturevalley.co.uk*
016974 73552.
Follow the walks through the woodland and countryside of this working dairy farm dotted with
sculptures. Try pond dipping or explore the play area. Open Thurs-Tues, 10.30am-5pm. Schools
Refreshments Open all year Price A.

Cockermouth, Lakeland Sheep & Wool Centre, *Egremont Road, 01900 822673.*
Come face to face with sheep during one of the indoor presentations, held four times a day. Sheep
shows run Mar-Oct, Sun-Thurs. Centre open daily, 9.30am-5.30pm. Schools Birthdays
Refreshments Open all year Price B.

Dalton-in-Furness, South Lakes Wild Animal Park, *Broughton Road,*
www.wildanimalpark.co.uk 01229 466086.
Home to a wide range of animals, big and small. Feed the kangaroos yourself and walk the tree-top
canopy with the lemurs. Safari railway, adventure play and picnic areas. Open daily, 10am-5pm
(4.30pm winter). Schools Birthdays **Refreshments Open all year Price D.**

Grange-over-Sands, Duckys Park Farm, *Moor Lane, Flookburgh, www.duckysparkfarm.co.uk*
015395 59293.
Get close to this farm's four-legged residents and learn about modern farming. Explore the farm-themed soft play area or test yourself on the roads of the driving school. Opening times vary, please check. Schools Birthdays **Refreshments Price B.**

Keswick, Trotters World of Animals, *Coalbeck Farm, Bassenthwaite, www.trottersworld.com*
017687 76239.
Learn about and handle an eclectic mix of animals, from otters to porcupines, from gibbons to snakes. See hawks and owls flying. Indoor and outdoor play areas. Open daily, summer, 10am-5.30pm, winter, 11am-4.30pm. Schools Birthdays **Open all year Price B.**

Lowther, Lakeland Bird of Prey Centre, *Lowther Castle, www.visitcumbria.com 01931 712746.*
A sanctuary for eagles, falcons, hawks and owls from around the world. Daily flying demonstrations and 'experience' days. Open Apr-Oct, daily from 11am, closing times vary. Groups **Refreshments Price B.**

Maryport, Lake District Coast Aquarium, *South Quay, www.lakedistrict-coastaquarium.co.uk*
01900 817760.
Get close to sea life native to Cumbria. Daily programme of activities and talks, and an opportunity to stroke the rays. Remote-controlled boats, adventure playground and miniature golf. Open daily, 10am-5pm. Schools Birthdays **Refreshments Open all year Price B.**

Milnthorpe, Lakeland Wildlife Oasis, *Hale, www.wildlifeoasis.co.uk 015395 63027.*
Follow evolution over 3,000 million years through interactive displays and animal handling. Walk in the tropical hall where butterflies and bats fly freely. Endangered species are kept as part of the international breeding programme. Open daily, Easter-Aug, 10am-5pm, Sept-Easter, 10am-4pm. Schools Birthdays **Refreshments Open all year Price B.**

Newby Bridge, Aquarium of the Lakes, *Lakeside, www.aquariumofthelakes.co.uk*
015395 30153.
Discover the wildlife above and below the lakes. See pike, British sharks and otters or explore 'Midnight at the Waters Edge'. Open daily, Apr-Oct, 9am-6pm, Nov-Mar, 9am-5pm. Schools Birthdays **Refreshments Open all year Price B.**

Penrith(near), The Alpaca Centre, *Snuff Mill Lane, Stainton, www.thealpacacentre.co.uk*
01768 891440.
A chance to see alpacas on this small farm which breeds and rears this unusual and surprisingly companionable animal. Open daily, 10am-5pm. **Refreshments Open all year Price A.**
Eden Ostrich World, *Langwathby Hall Farm, Langwathby, www.ostrich-world.com 01768 881771.*
Allow at least two hours to visit this working farm with lots of activities. You may be lucky enough to witness the amazing sight of ostrich chicks hatching and children will love to stroke the baby animals in pets corner. See many rare breeds and watch the sheep at milking time. Take a riverside walk or enjoy the large traffic-free play area. Daily programme of events during school holidays and weekends. Picnic area and indoor play area. Open daily, Mar-Oct, 10am-5pm, Nov-Feb, Wed-Mon. Schools Birthdays **Refreshments Open all year Price B Check out page 38.**

Sedbergh, Holme Open Farm, *www.holmeopenfarm.co.uk 015396 20654.*
Regular farm tours, nature trail, demonstrations and baby animals to feed in spring. Events daily. An evening badger watch starts at dusk, telephone for details. Open daily, Mar-Sept, 11am-4pm. Schools **Price A.**

FREE PLACES

Hadrian's Wall World Heritage Site, *www.hadrianswallcountry.org 01434 322002.*
This famous frontier was built by order of the Roman Emperor Hadrian. Along its length are many museums, forts and temples. Follow the National Trail – Hadrian's Wall Path, an 84-mile trail from coast to coast with links to 40 short walks.

The Lake District is the largest of England's National Parks and offers stunning scenery, a mixture of lakes and mountains. Walking is without doubt one of the most popular ways to explore, from challenging hill walking to one of the many trails along the shores of the lakes. Tourist Information Centres are a great source of information from which you can plan a family outing.

Ambleside, The Homes of Football, *100 Lake Road, www.homesoffootball.co.uk 015394 34440.*
Happiness for any football fan, this unique collection of photographs captures the spirit of the game. You are sure to find your team amongst the displays. Open daily, Apr-Aug, 10am-5pm, Sept-Mar, Wed-Mon. Groups **Open all year.**

Barrow-in-Furness, The Dock Museum, *North Road, www.dockmuseum.org.uk 01229 894444.*
Built over a Victorian dock, this museum explores the history of shipbuilding and its impact on the town. Fantastic displays, re-creations and a themed adventure playground. Opening days and times vary, please ring. Schools Refreshments **Open all year.**

Braithwaite, Whinlatter Forest Park, *www.forestry.gov.uk 017687 78469.*
Spend a day in this mountain forest that has a badger's set, family walks, orienteering, playground and picnic area. See live footage of the ospreys in summer. Events and activities. Park open daily until dusk. Visitor centre open daily from 10am, closing times vary. Schools Refreshments **Open all year.**

Brampton(near), Haweswater, *www.rspb.co.uk 01931 713376.*
Watch golden eagles on their nest – this is the only place in the UK where you can. The path to the observation point is uneven so is most suitable for older children. Take binoculars for a rare sight. Observation point open Apr-Aug, 11am-4pm. Groups **Open all year Check out RSPB on pages 63 and 64.**

Carlisle(near), Eden Benchmarks, *East Cumbria Countryside Project, www.edenarts.co.uk 01228 561601.*
This is a unique collection of ten stone sculptures placed at different locations along the length of the River Eden. **Open all year.**

Hawkshead, Grizedale Forest Park, *www.forestry.gov.uk 01229 860010.*
Look out for the famous forest sculptures and follow the waymarked trails. Picnic areas, visitor centre and playground. See Go Ape! in 'Adventure' section. Visitor centre open daily from 10am, closing times vary. Schools Refreshments **Open all year.**

Keswick, Castlerigg Stone Circle, *EH, 0191 269 1214.*
Dating from around 3000 BC, the circle is 30 metres in diameter and contains 38 stones, the tallest of which is 2.3m in height. An interesting site and great for a picnic. Open any reasonable time, check for details. **Open all year.**

Keswick Museum and Art Gallery, *Fitz Park, Station Road, www.allerdale.gov.uk 017687 73263.*
Set in parkland, this museum charts the history of the area from its discovery as a holiday destination to its mining heritage. There are musical stones, letters from Wordsworth and a 500-year-old cat to discover. Open Easter-Oct, Tues-Sat, 10am-4pm. Groups

Lindal in Furness, Colony Country Store, *www.colonicalcandles.com 01229 461102.*
Visit the exhibition centre and learn all about candle making and the history of the area, or have a go and dip your own (telephone for details). Open Mon-Sat, 9am-5pm, Sun, 10.30am-4.30pm. Groups Refreshments **Open all year.**

Newby Bridge, Fell Foot Park, NT, *015395 31273.*
A restored Victorian Park with an adventure playground, rowing boat hire and picnic areas. Programme of children's activities throughout the year. Open daily, 9am-5pm or dusk if earlier. Groups **Refreshments Open all year.**

Penrith, Penrith Museum, *Robinson's School, Middlegate, www.visitcumbria.com 01768 212228.*
Examine the history of Penrith and the Eden Valley in this old school building. Changing exhibitions, telephone for details. Open Mon-Sat, 10am-4pm. Schools **Open all year.**
Rheged, *Redhills, www.rheged.com 01768 868000.*
Watch chocolates being made or enjoy a large-format movie on the giant cinema screen. There is also the Helly Hansen National Mountaineering Exhibition and a soft play area for younger children. Admission charge for some activities. Open daily, 10am-5.30pm. Schools Birthdays **Refreshments Open all year Price P.**
Wetheriggs Pottery, *Clifton Dykes, www.wetheriggs-pottery.co.uk 01768 892733.*
Try your hand at throwing your own pot or paint a pot or plate (charges apply) at the UK's last steam-powered pottery. Children's play area. Ring to book pottery during busy holiday periods. Open daily, 10am-5.30pm. Groups Birthdays **Refreshments Open all year.**

Penrith(near), Abbott Lodge Jersey Ice Cream, *Clifton www.abbottlodgejerseyicecream.co.uk 01931 712720.*
A working dairy farm where you can see the Jersey cows, try the ice cream or run around in the indoor and outdoor playgrounds. Open daily, Easter-Oct, 11am-5pm; Nov-Easter, Sat-Sun and Tues-Thurs. Schools Birthdays **Refreshments Open all year.**
Aira Force Waterfall, NT, *01768 482067.*
A magnificent beauty spot and the starting point for many walks and nature trails. Aira Force and the surrounding countryside are home to a large variety of birds, mammals, insects, flowers and reptiles. Groups **Open all year.**

Sellafield, Sellafield Visitors Centre, *Seascale, www.go-experimental.com 01946 727027.*
Budding scientists of all ages can 'Go experi-MENTAL' at the Sellafield Visitors Centre. It's fascinating and fun too. Use the children's excess energy to jump up and down for power. Meet the professor at the hourly science shows at weekends and school holidays. Experiment with electricity, gravity and magnetism. Discover the Top Secret Science Labs, which are packed with interactive experiments that make learning fun – and you can even try some of them at home. If you're looking for extra thrills, dare to visit the Immersion Cinema, where you get to control the Earth's environment and ultimately, the destiny of the dinosaurs. Open daily, Apr-Oct, 10am-5pm, Nov-Mar, 10am-4pm. Schools Birthdays **Refreshments Open all year Check out page 38.**

Sizergh, Low Sizergh Barn, *www.lowsizerghbarn.co.uk 015395 60426.*
Follow the farm trail at this organic dairy farm and watch the milking from the tearoom gallery after 4pm. Picnic area and large organic produce shop. Open daily, Easter-Christmas, 9am-5.30pm, Christmas-Easter, 9.30am-5pm. **Refreshments Open all year.**

Whitehaven, Haig Colliery Mining Museum, *Solway Road, Kells, www.haigpit.com 01946 599949.*
Learn about life down the mines for children in Victorian times and about working in the 1950s. Hands-on activities. Open daily, 9.30am-4.30pm. Schools **Open all year.**

Windermere, Lake District Visitor Centre, *Brockhole, www.lake-district.co.uk 015394 46601.*
Interactive exhibitions teach children about Lakeland life. Hourly boat trips to Ambleside from the lake shore. Adventure playground and pitch and putt golf. Open daily, Mar-Oct, 10am-5pm. Schools Birthdays **Refreshments.**

Alston, Alston Model Railway Centre, *Station Yard Workshops, 01434 382100.*
Watch the permanent exhibition of model railway layouts including a hands-on layout for children. Open daily, Easter-Oct, 11am-5pm, Nov-Easter, Wed-Mon, 11am-4pm. Groups **Open all year** Price A.

Ambleside, Lakes Discovery Museum at the Armitt, *Rydal Road, www.armitt.com*
015394 31212.
Discover history from Roman times to the present, together with Beatrix Potter's natural history water colours. Family events, children's guides, hands-on activities and work sheets. Open daily, 10am-5pm. Schools **Open all year** Price A.

Bowness–on-Windermere, Blackwell – The Arts & Crafts House, *www.blackwell.org.uk*
015394 46139.
An historic house and garden with spectacular views across Windermere and restored interiors furnished with period furniture. Original features include stained glass windows, decorative plasterwork, carved oak panelling and stonework. Open daily, 15th Feb-24th Dec, 10.30am-5pm; Feb, Mar, Nov, Dec, closes 4pm. Schools **Refreshments** Price B.

The World of Beatrix Potter Attraction, *The Old Laundry, www.hop-skip-jump.com*
015394 88444.
See the characters brought to life at this enchanting indoor re-creation of the tales of Beatrix Potter. There are new characters and bigger exhibitions following recent redevelopment. Open daily, 21st Mar-Sept, 10am-5.30pm, Oct-Mar, 10am-4.30pm. Groups **Refreshments Open all year** Price B.

Cark-in-Cartmel, Holker Hall and Gardens & The Lakeland Motor Museum,
www.holker-hall.co.uk 015395 58328.
Enjoy this stately home and award-winning gardens together with the Motor Museum and Campbell Bluebird Legend Exhibition. Picnic area, adventure playground, children's guides and family activities in school holidays. Opening times and days vary, ring for details. Schools Birthdays **Refreshments** Price C.

Carlisle, Alice's Wonderland, *Highhead Farm, Ivegill, www.alices-wonderland.co.uk*
016974 73025.
A personal collection of dolls, houses, teddies, prams and all things miniature, with some pieces dating from around 1800. Children are encouraged to explore and play. Open Thurs-Tues, 10.30am-5pm. Schools Birthdays **Refreshments Open all year** Price A.

Carlisle Castle, EH, *01228 591922.*
Examine the dungeon's 1480 graffiti or the 'licking stones' where parched prisoners drank. Mary, Queen of Scots was imprisoned here. Guided tours available by arrangement. Ticket includes entry to the Regiment Museum (see below). Open daily, Apr-Sept, 9.30am-6pm, Oct-Mar, 10am-4pm. Schools **Open all year** Price B.

King's Own Royal Border Regiment Museum, *Queen Mary's Tower, The Castle,*
www.armymuseums.org.uk 01228 532774.
Wide-ranging displays include uniforms, equipment, anti-tank guns and other weapons. Look out for the 103-year-old box of chocolates! Entry included in Carlisle Castle admission. Open daily, Apr-Sept, 9.30am-6pm, Oct-Mar, 10am-4pm. Schools **Open all year** Price B.

The Solway Aviation Museum, *Aviation House, Carlisle Airport, Crosby-on-Eden,*
www.solway-aviation-museum.co.uk 01228 573823.
Sit in the pilot's seat, work in the control tower and visit the many jets on display. Experience the new night vision exhibit for 2006. Open Apr-Oct. Sat-Sun and Bank Hols, 10.30am-5pm, also Mon & Fri during school hols. Schools **Price A.**

Tullie House Museum and Art Gallery, *Castle Street, www.tulliehouse.co.uk 01228 534781.*
Discover the history of Carlisle and the Roman Empire. Exciting re-creations, hands-on activities and audiovisual displays. Events programme with family activities during school holidays. Opening times vary. Schools **Refreshments Open all year** Price B.

Cockermouth, Cumberland Toy & Model Museum, *Banks Court, Market Place, www.toymuseum.co.uk 01900 827606.*
The museum evokes childhood memories for young and old, with toys from the 1900s through to the present day. Press the buttons to see the toys work. Please telephone for opening times. Schools **Open all year** Price A.

Coniston, Brantwood, *www.brantwood.org.uk 015394 41396.*
The home of John Ruskin, artist and writer, has a hands-on den with painting materials. Ruskin's boat and coach are on display and the original ice house can be seen. Open daily, mid Mar-mid Nov, 11am-5.30pm, winter, Wed-Sun, 11am-4.30pm. Schools **Refreshments Open all year** Price B.

The Ruskin Museum, *www.ruskinmuseum.com 015394 41164.*
Find out about Donald Campbell's water speed record, Coniston Water, the geology of the area and local artist John Ruskin. Interactive computers and hands-on exhibitions. Open daily, mid Mar-mid Nov, 10am-5.30pm, winter, Wed-Sun, 10.30am-3.30pm. Schools **Open all year** Price A.

Egremont, Florence Mine Heritage Centre, *www.florencemine.co.uk 01946 825830.*
Take a tour around a working iron-ore mine. Learn about mining and miners' lives in the Heritage Centre. Suitable clothing and footwear required. Open Mon-Fri, 9.30am-3.30pm, Apr-Oct, Sat, Sun & Bank Hol Mons, 10am-4pm. Schools **Open all year** Price C.

Finsthwaite, Stott Park Bobbin Mill, EH, *01539 531087.*
Watch bobbins being produced on restored machinery. A working museum, giving a taste of industrial life and working conditions for the Victorian bobbin makers. Guided tours and events. Open daily, Apr-Sept, 10am-6pm, Oct, 10am-5pm. Schools **Price A.**

Gilsland, Birdoswald Roman Fort, *www.birdoswaldromanfort.org 016977 47602.*
Explore this well-preserved stretch of Hadrian's Wall, once home to 1,000 Roman soldiers. Interactive visitor centre and special events programme. Open daily, Mar-Oct, 10am-5.30pm. Schools **Refreshments Price A.**

Holmbrook(near), Eskdale Mill, *Boot Village, 019467 23335.*
Visit one of the oldest working two-wheeled, water-powered corn mills nestling in the foothills of Scafell. Oatmeal milled daily. Why not take a picnic to the impressive waterfalls which power the mill? Open Easter-Sept, Sun-Fri, 11am-5pm. Schools **Price A.**

Kendal, Abbot Hall, *www.abbothall.org.uk 01539 722464.*
This small independent art gallery displays both old and modern works. Changing programme of exhibitions and activities, with a Saturday Art Club and family boxes to help young children understand the exhibits. Open mid Jan-mid Dec, Mon-Sat, 10.30am-5pm (4pm in winter). Schools **Refreshments Price B.**

Kendal Museum, *Station Road, www.kendalmuseum.org.uk 01539 721374.*
With fossil rubbing and a computer interactive display of Kendal Castle, there is lots to see and do here. Activities include workshops during school holidays. Open Mon-Sat, mid Feb-Mar & Nov-Dec, 10.30am-4pm, Apr-Oct, 10.30am-5pm. Schools **Price A.**

Levens Hall, *www.levenshall.co.uk 015395 60321.*
Historic Elizabethan family home with lovely gardens including a fabulous topiary. Children's quiz book and adventure playground. Steam engine and model traction engine most Sundays. Open early Apr-mid Oct, Sun-Thurs. Gardens, 10am-5pm. House, 12noon-5pm. Schools **Price B** (Gardens only) **Price C** (House & Gardens).

Museum of Lakeland Life, *Abbot Hall, www.lakelandmuseum.org.uk 01539 722464.*
Discover how Cumbrians have worked, lived and entertained themselves for the last 200 years.
Visit re-created Lakeland room settings and learn about Cumbria's unique history. Events and
activities programme. Open mid Jan-mid Dec, Mon-Sat, 10.30am-5pm (4pm winter). Schools
Refreshments Price B.

Keswick, Cars of the Stars Museum, *Standish Street, www.carsofthestars.com 017687 73757.*
Can you find your favourites? Chitty Chitty Bang Bang, Mr Bean's Mini, Harry Potter's Ford Anglia
and many, many more. Open daily, Easter-Nov & Feb school hols, 10am-5pm, Dec, Sat-Sun.
Schools Price B.

Cumberland Pencil Museum, *Southey Works, Greta Bridge, www.pencils.co.uk 017687 73626.*
Learn about the history of pencil making and see the world's longest pencil. Do you know how
the lead gets inside? Children's drawing corner and drawing competitions. Open daily, 9.30am-
4pm. Extended opening during school hols. Schools **Open all year** Price A.

Mirehouse, *www.mirehouse.com 017687 72287.*
Award-winning historic home and gardens. Look out for the schoolroom and nursery, enjoy the
Poetry Walk and the Bee Garden. Natural adventure playground, children's history trail and nature
notes. Open Apr-Oct. Gardens daily, 10am-5.30pm. House, Sun, Wed (& Fri in Aug), 2-5pm.
Schools Refreshments Price B.

The Puzzling Place, *Museum Square, www.puzzlingplace.co.uk 017687 75102.*
Fascinated or frustrated? Can you work out how water flows uphill in the Anti-Gravity Room or
will the Optical Illusions blow your mind? Hands-on Puzzle Area and much more. Open daily,
10am-6pm. Schools Birthdays **Open all year** Price A.

Threlkeld Quarry & Mining Museum, *Threlkeld Quarry, www.threlkeldminingmuseum.co.uk
017687 79747.*
Discover the history of mining, from hand chipping to huge modern earth-moving processes, and
have a go at panning for minerals! Underground tour not suitable for under 4s, dress sensibly.
Open daily, Easter-Oct, including all Bank Hols (weather permitting), 10am-5pm. Schools Price C.

Keswick(near), Honister Slate Mine, *Honister Pass, www.honister.com 017687 77230.*
Take the Big Mountain Mine Tour deep underground and learn about the traditional skills of slate
mining or spend time in the Visitors Centre. Three tours daily, ring for details. Mountain buggies
available for small children. Open Mon-Fri, 9am-5pm, Sat, Sun & Bank Hols, 10am-5pm. Schools
Open all year Price C.

Maryport, Senhouse Roman Museum, *The Battery, Sea Brows, www.senhousemuseum.co.uk
01900 816168.*
Follow 'Humphrey's Guide', dress up as a Roman or take part in an archaeological dig. Events
programme with workshops during school holidays. Open Apr-Jun, Tues, Thurs-Sun, 10am-5pm;
Jul-Oct & Bank Hols, daily, 10am-5pm; Nov-Mar, Fri-Sun, 10.30am-4pm. Schools **Open all year**
Price A.

Milnthorpe, Heron Corn Mill and the Museum of Paper Making, *Beetham,
www.heronmill.org 015395 65027.*
This restored working mill displays the mechanics of a water-powered corn mill. The museum
explains the process of paper making and has art activities and workshops throughout the year.
Open Mar-Oct, Tues-Sun, 11am-5pm. Schools Price A.

Nenthead, Nenthead Mines Heritage Centre, *www.npht.com 01434 382037.*
Experience 'The Power of Water and Darkness' at Nenthead. Pan for minerals and dare to stand
on top of a 100-metre mine shaft. Height and age restrictions apply for mine visits. Open Easter-
Oct, Wed-Sun, 10.30am-5pm, and daily during school hols. Schools Refreshments Price B.

Penrith, Dalemain Historic House & Gardens, *www.dalemain.com 017684 86450.*
A spectacular family home - look out for Mrs Mouse's House and the nursery. Outside, see fallow deer, red squirrels and the children's garden. Open 26th Mar-29th Oct, Sun-Thurs, Gardens, 10.30am-5pm, House, 11am-4pm; winter (Gardens only), Sun-Thurs, 11am-4pm.   Schools Refreshments **Price A.**

Penrith(near), Brougham Castle, EH, *01768 862488.*
See the ruins of this impressive historical site. Imagine what life was like living at the castle and study the exhibition of relics from Roman times. Open daily, Apr-Sept, 10am-6pm, Oct, 10am-4pm. Schools **Price A.**

Hutton-in-the-Forest, *www.hutton-in-the-forest.co.uk 01768 484449.*
Explore this richly furnished historic house using children's quiz sheets (available school and Bank Hols). Visit the walled gardens and enjoy the woodland walk. Open Easter-Oct. Gardens, Sun-Wed, 11am-5pm. House, Wed, Thurs, Sun & Bank Hol Mons, 12.30-4pm.   Schools Refreshments **Price B.**

Ravenglass, The Muncaster Experience, *Muncaster Castle, www.muncaster.co.uk 01229 717614.*
This castle offers a great family day out, see the indoor Meadow Vole Maze and the World Owl Centre, which holds a daily flying display at 2.30pm. Outdoor play area. Open 13th Feb-6th Nov, times vary. Schools Refreshments **Price C.**

Silloth-on-Solway, Solway Coast Discovery Centre, *Liddell Street, www.solwaycoastaonb.org.uk 016973 31944.*
Meet 'Auld Michael' the monk and 'Oyk' the Oystercatcher. Learn about the 40-year history of this Area of Outstanding Natural Beauty and its formation in the Ice Age. Time Machine exhibition. Open daily, Apr-Oct, 10am-4pm; telephone for winter opening. Schools **Open all year Price A.**

Sizergh, Sizergh Castle, NT, *015395 60070.*
A family home dating from medieval times and noted for its interior decoration. The estate includes a rock garden and woodlands. Events programme and children's quiz sheet for both house and gardens. Open Easter-Oct, Sun-Thurs. Gardens from 12.30pm, House, 1.30-5pm. Schools Refreshments **Price B.**

Troutbeck, Townend, NT, *015394 32628.*
This 17th century family home contains books, furniture and domestic implements from the past. Children can help to make a rag rug and meet 'Mr Brown' as part of the living history programme most Thursdays. Open Easter-Oct, Wed-Sun, 1-4.30pm or dusk if earlier. Schools **Price A.**

Ulverston, Laurel and Hardy Museum, *Upper Brook Street, www.laurel-and-hardy-museum.co.uk 01229 582292.*
Housed in Stan Laurel's birth-town of Ulverston, this museum is dedicated to the famous comedians. See the large collection of memorabilia including letters and personal items. A cinema shows films and documentaries. Open daily, Feb-Dec, 10am-4.30pm. Groups **Price A.**

Ulverston(near), Gleaston Water Mill, *Gleaston, www.watermill.co.uk 01229 869244.*
A restored, working water-powered corn mill with observation beehive. Small collection of farm animals. Events and activities throughout the year. Open Tues-Sun, 10.30am-5pm. Schools Refreshments **Open all year Price A.**

Whitehaven, The Beacon, *West Strand, www.thebeacon-whitehaven.co.uk 0845 095 2131.*
Become a TV weatherman. The Beacon holds the Met Office Gallery where hands-on displays and interactive computers explain world weather systems. Programme of activities. Open Easter-Oct, Tues-Sun, 10am-5.30pm, and Mons in school hols & Bank Hols; Nov-Easter, Tues-Sun, 10am-4.30pm. Groups Refreshments **Open all year Price B.**

The Rum Story, *Lowther Street, www.rumstory.co.uk 01946 592933.*
Learn about rum making and its history - smuggling, prohibition and slavery are all part of the story. See the re-created rain forest and African village. Open daily, 10am-4.30pm.   Schools Birthdays **Open all year Price B.**

Windermere, Windermere Steamboat and Museum, *Rayrigg Road, www.steamboat.co.uk 015394 45565.*
View a special collection of steam and motor boats, set in a striking lakeside location. Model boat pond and picnic area. Special events, cruises and art exhibitions. Open daily, mid Mar-early Nov, 10am-5pm.   Schools **Refreshments Price A.**

TRIPS & TRANSPORT

BOAT TRIPS

Coniston, Coniston Launch, *www.conistonlaunch.co.uk 015394 36216.*
Departures from a number of points around the lake. Special interest cruises include 'Swallows and Amazons' and 'Campbells on Coniston' on selected dates. Sailings all year with a limited service Nov-Mar. Groups **Open all year Price P.**
Steam Yacht Gondola, *NT, 015394 41288.*
This restored Victorian boat is also available for private charter. Sailings daily, Apr-Oct. Groups Birthdays **Price B.**

Derwentwater, Keswick Launch, *www.keswick-launch.co.uk 017687 72263.*
A full timetable of trips around the lake from different stages. Private charter available. Sailings daily, mid Mar-Nov; Dec-mid Mar, Sat-Sun. Groups Birthdays **Open all year Price P.**

Ullswater, Ullswater Steamers, *www.ullswater-steamers.co.uk 017684 82229.*
Cruises from various stages around the lake and with a selection of themes. Sailings throughout the year, times vary. Groups **Open all year Price P.**

Windermere, Windermere Lake Cruises, *www.windermere-lakecruises.co.uk 015395 31188.*
Enjoy a variety of trips departing from Lakeside, Bowness or Ambleside. Combined cruise and attraction tickets available. Sailings all year, reduced service Nov-Easter. Groups **Open all year Price P.**

TRAIN TRIPS

Alston, South Tynedale Railway, *www.strps.org.uk 01434 381696 (talking timetable 01434 382828).*
Travel over two miles by steam on this narrow-gauge railway to Kirkhaugh. Take a walk and enjoy the scenery before the return trip. Phone for opening times. Groups **Refreshments Price B.**

Ravenglass, Ravenglass to Eskdale Railway, *www.ravenglass-railway.co.uk 01229 717171.*
Venture seven miles into the heart of the Eskdale Valley. Find out about 'La'al Ratty', the water vole stationmaster, and look for his quiz book. 'Santa Trains' before Christmas. Operates daily, mid Mar-Oct; limited service Nov-mid Mar. Schools Birthdays **Refreshments Open all year Price C.**

Settle, Settle to Carlisle Railway Line, *www.settle-carlisle.co.uk 0870 602 3322.*
Regarded as one of the country's most scenic train journeys, this service runs daily, stopping at various stations in Cumbria and Yorkshire. For details on occasional steam charter phone 09065 660 607. Groups **Open all year Price P.**

Ulverston, Lakeside & Haverthwaite Railway, *Haverthwaite Station, 015395 31594.*
A trip by steam locomotive along this steeply graded line running through beautiful countryside. Operates daily, mid Apr-Oct. Groups **Price B.**

Can't find a babysitter?

SitterS
0800 38 900 38

For Evening Babysitters
www.sitters.co.uk

Evening Babysitters with Professional Childcare Experience

Now you can find mature, friendly and reliable evening babysitters, available at short notice. For your reassurance we interview each babysitter in person and check all references thoroughly.

All Sitters babysitters have professional childcare experience and most are local authority registered childminders or professionally qualified nursery nurses.

How does Sitters' service work

When you make a booking we arrange for a babysitter to attend at the appointed time. At the end of the evening you pay the babysitter for the hours they have worked. Babysitting rates are competitive and vary depending on your area - please phone for details. There are no additional charges for travelling costs and all bookings are for a minimum of 4 hours.

Each time you book a babysitter we charge you a nominal booking fee to your credit card. You can register with Sitters free! Membership of just £12.75 for 3 months will only be charged after your first sitting. Call us today - less than £1 per week is a small price to ensure your children are in experienced hands.

Experienced Childcarers Needed

Sitters welcomes applications from suitable babysitters. You will need to be over 21, have professional childcare experience, your own transport and immaculate references. For more information and to register your interest, phone 0800 38 900 38 or visit www.sitters.co.uk.

For more information, phone us FREE today or

0800 38 900 38
or visit us at www.sitters.co.uk

Please quote Ref: LET'S GO

RE C
Recruitment & Employment Confederation

We're in YELLOW PAGES

INVESTOR IN PEOPLE

Greater Manchester

O ne of Britain's largest metropolitan conurbations, with more football teams per head of population than any other city in the world! The legacy left by the 2002 Commonwealth Games is some of the best sporting facilities in the country (see the 'Sports & Leisure' chapter). The area is also famous for its industrial and social heritage, which is celebrated in many of Manchester's museums and galleries. City centre Manchester is now considered to be one of the 'coolest' places for shopping, eating and entertainment.

ADVENTURE, FUN & SOFT PLAY

Chadderton, Fun Bay 1, *Watts Street, 0161 620 5955.*
Spy on your parents seated below as you traverse the aerial rope bridges around the room. Bouncy castle, slides and ball ponds, as well as a separate toddler village. Open daily from 10am, closing times vary. Groups Birthdays **Refreshments Open all year** Price A.

Cheadle, Funizuz, *Brookfield Industrial Estate, Brookfield Road, 0161 491 6611.*
Will you race down the two-lane astroslide or over the scramble nets? There is plenty of space here for both children and adults, plus a safe toddler area. Open daily, 10am-6pm. Groups Birthdays **Refreshments Open all year** Price A.

Dukinfield, KK5, *Wharf Street, www.kinderkeyplaycentres.co.uk 0161 339 4491.*
Speed down the freefall drop slides or swing on the aerial glides. Rope bridges, ball ponds and scramble nets complete the fun. Open daily from 10am, closing times vary. Groups Birthdays **Refreshments Open all year** Price A.

Dunham Massey, Redhouse Farm, *Redhouse Lane, www.redhousefarm.co.uk 0161 941 3480.*
Looking for some summer excitement? Fancy immersing yourself in an Aztec Adventure? Get lost in this uniquely designed maze as you hunt for Aztec treasure with the 'Quest for the Golden Cob'. Once you've succeeded, relax and enjoy the numerous courtyard attractions to complete your energetic family day out. As the nights draw in, Redhouse Farm takes on a more spooky atmos-fear as they host their annual Halloween 'Spooktacular'. With 'The Creepy Cottage', 'The Beast' and new for 2006, the 'Field of Screams'. Family entertainment doesn't get more thrilling! Maze open daily, mid Jul-mid Sept, 10am–6pm. Spooktacular open daily through October half term, 12noon–8pm. Schools Birthdays **Refreshments** Price B **Check out page 50.**

Hyde, Hyde Leisure Pool, *Walker Lane, www.tameside.gov.uk 0161 368 4057.*
Dare you try the white water ride through the tunnel? Splash down the slide and jump in the waves. The pool also has a jacuzzi, water beds and fountains. Open daily, times vary. Groups Birthdays **Refreshments Open all year** Price B.

Jumping Jacks Adventureland, *Caxon works, Dukinfield Road, 0161 366 9366.*
Home to Turbo Jacks (go-karting for 6-12 year olds), Jumping Jacks soft play and Cactus Jacks Wild West Action Town for all ages. Open Tues-Sun, and Mon during school hols, 10am, closing times vary. Groups Birthdays **Refreshments Open all year** Price P.

Manchester, Laser Quest, *Parrs Wood Entertainment Complex, Wilmslow Road, www.laserquest.co.uk 0161 445 0687.*
Strap on the equipment and prepare for laser games in a space-age adventure. Open Mon-Fri, 4-10pm, Sat, Sun & school hols, 10am-10pm. Groups Birthdays **Refreshments Open all year** Price A.

Oldham, Jolly Jungle, *Featherstall Road, 0161 628 4411.*
Indoor adventure play centre with separate baby and toddler areas. Messy activities for pre-school children, Mon-Fri, 10am-2pm. Open daily from 9.30am, closing times vary. Groups Birthdays **Refreshments Open all year** Price A.

REDHOUSE FARM
Dunham Massey

is **the** place in the Greater Manchester region for providing on-farm entertainment.

The summer Maize Maze and the Halloween Spooktacular allows kids of all ages to play, learn, grow & scream!

Maize maze runs Mid July to Mid September	Halloween spooktacular runs through the October Half term, call for more details

Redhouse Farm, Redhouse Lane, Dunham Massey, Altrincham, WA14 5RL
www.redhousefarm.co.uk - info@redhousefarm.co.uk - 07766 770069

Smithills Open Farm

Smithills Dean Road
Bolton, Lancs BL1 7NS
Tel: 01204 595765
Fax: 01204 461042
email: info@smithillsopenfarm.co.uk
web: www.smithillsopenfarm.co.uk

A Family Run Business
Where the children have the time of their lives!

Opening times:
Tuesday to Sunday 10:30am to 5:00pm
Closed Mondays (except School & Bank Holidays)
Additional visits by appointment

Come early and stay all day!

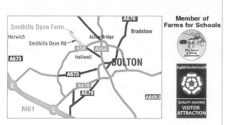

Member of
Farms for Schools

Poynton, Brookside Garden Centre & Miniature Railway, *Macclesfield Road, www.brookside-miniature-railway.co.uk 01625 872919.*
A steam miniature railway runs half a mile around the garden centre, through level crossings, stations and past signal boxes. Operates most weekends, times vary with season. **Refreshments Open all year Price P.**

Reddish, Whale Around, *Houldsworth Mill, Houldsworth Street, www.whalearound.com 0161 432 4020.*
A pirate ship-themed soft play area. Under 4s can try cars whilst older children have two levels of fun to explore. Check out the fish in the aquarium. Open Mon-Sat, 9.30am-6pm, Sun, 11am-5pm. Closed Bank Hols. Groups Birthdays **Refreshments Open all year Price A.**

Royton, Play Oldham, *Laurel Trading Estate, Higginshaw Lane, www.playoldham.com 0161 627 3000.*
Race down the three-lane astroslide to find a winner. A three-tier play area with plenty of space. Open Mon-Wed, 10am-6pm, Thurs-Sat, 10am-7pm, Sun, 10am-4pm. Groups Birthdays **Refreshments Open all year Price A.**
Sparkles Adventure Play, *Market Square, 0161 628 5530.*
Enter this fantasy castle in the centre of town with three tiers of play equipment. Watch the children from the comfort of the mezzanine floor. Open Mon-Sat, 10am-6pm, Sun, 10am-4pm. Groups Birthdays **Refreshments Open all year Price A.**

Stockport, KK5, *King Street West, www.kinderkeyplaycentres.co.uk 0161 477 2225.*
Kings and Queens can explore three levels of fun, with toddlers having a kitchen and Wendy house to enjoy. Cool down in the TV area afterwards. Open daily from 10am, closing times vary. Groups Birthdays **Refreshments Open all year Price A.**
Rumble in the Jungle, *Hallam Street, Heaviley, 0161 477 8438.*
Explorers can trek through this jungle themed soft play area - dive into ball pools or climb rope bridges. Separate areas designed especially for babies, and car zone for little drivers and bike riders. An art and craft area offers a quieter zone. Younger children can enjoy Jungle Tots sessions from 9.30am-12noon each weekday, with organised activities daily. Open daily, 9.30am-5.30pm. Groups Birthdays **Refreshments Open all year Price A.**
The Trafford Centre, *www.traffordcentre.co.uk 0161 749 1717.*
Inside one of the largest shopping malls in the North West you will find a 17-screen cinema, Laser Quest tag game, climbing wall and large soft play area with creche facilities. Ring for opening times and prices. **Refreshments Open all year Price P.**

FARMS, WILDLIFE & NATURE PARKS

Bolton, Smithills Open Farm, *Smithills Dean Road, www.smithillsopenfarm.co.uk 01204 595765.*
Set in the vast open countryside of Smithills Country Park next to the historic Smithills Hall and Restaurant. Enjoy pony and donkey rides and holding the ducklings, chicks and baby rabbits in the pets corner. Feed the young lambs, calves and hens, see the llamas, owls and other birds or help milk the cows! Pretend to be a farmer on the toy tractor and trailer or have fun on the adventure walks and play areas, which include a bouncy castle. Open mid Feb-Christmas, Tues-Sun, 10.30am-5pm, open Bank Hol Mons and daily in school holidays. Schools Birthdays **Refreshments Price B Check out page 50.**

Stockport, Roman Lakes Leisure Park, *www.romanlakes.co.uk 0161 427 2039.*
This beautiful countryside with river, canal and viaduct also offers bike hire, canoeing, playground and nature trails. Open daily, 8am-dusk. **Refreshments Open all year Price P.**

FREE PLACES

Ashton-under-Lyne, Central Art Gallery, *Old Street, www.tameside.gov.uk 0161 342 2650.*
A varied and changing exhibition programme, often showing the work of local artists. Children's activities and workshops during school holidays. Open Tues-Wed & Fri, 10am-12.30pm & 1-5pm, Thurs, 1-7.30pm, Sat, 9am-12.30pm & 1-4pm. Schools **Open all year.**

Museum of the Manchester Regiment, *Old Town Hall, Market Place, www.tameside.gov.uk 0161 342 3710.*
Displays and interactive exhibits tell this military story. Visitors can try on a soldier's headdress or experience a First World War trench. Activity sheets for children on request. Open Mon-Sat, 10am-4pm. Schools **Open all year.**

Park Bridge Heritage Centre, *The Stables, Park Bridge, 0161 330 9613.*
Follow the trail around the Medlock Valley and discover the area's industrial heritage and local wildlife. Exhibitions and great countryside events programme. Park open daily. Visitor centre open, Wed-Thurs & Sat-Sun, 11am-4pm. Schools **Open all year.**

Portland Basin Museum, *Portland Place, www.tameside.gov.uk 0161 343 2878.*
Join in with family-friendly activities in a canal-side setting. Learn about clog making, how lock gates work and playground games from yesteryear. Events programme and fun days. Open Tues-Sun & Bank Hol Mons, 10am-5pm. Schools **Open all year.**

Setantii, *Town Hall Building, www.tameside.gov.uk 0161 342 2812.*
A walk-through museum telling the story of the area from Celtic times to the present. Events and activities during school holidays. Open Mon-Fri, 10am-4pm, Sat, 10am-1pm. Schools **Open all year.**

Bolton, Bolton Museum Art Gallery and Aquarium, *Le Mans Crescent, www.boltonmuseum.org.uk 01204 332211.*
Find out about natural history and Egyptology or see the underwater world. Events programme with activities and workshops all year. Open Mon-Sat, 9am-5pm (closed Bank Hol Mons). Schools **Open all year.**

The Elephant Walk, *Bolton Tourist Information Centre, 01204 334321.*
Discover how many elephants you can spot on this walking trail around the town centre - you will be surprised how many you can see! **Open all year.**

Jumbles Country Park, *off Bradshaw Road, Bradshaw, www.visit-bolton.com 01204 853360.*
Take a picnic and follow the circular trail around the reservoir, looking out for the different birds, trees and plants. Ranger service and information centre. Park open daily. Schools Refreshments **Open all year.**

Moses Gate Country Park, *Hall Lane, Farnworth, www.croal-irwellvalley.co.uk 01204 334343.*
Meander around one of the waymarked trails, or feed the ducks and swans on one of the three large lakes. Ranger service with events programme. Visitor centre open daily, 9.30am-4.30pm. Schools **Open all year.**

Moss Bank Park, *Moss Bank Way, Halliwell, www.bolton.org.uk 01204 334050.*
A traditional town park with play area, miniature steam railway most Sundays and Bank Hols, Animal World and butterfly house. Events and fun days. Park open daily until dusk. Animal World open daily, Apr-Sept, 10am-4.30pm, Oct-Mar, Sat-Thurs, 10am-3.30pm, Fri, 10am-2.30pm. Schools Refreshments **Open all year.**

Bury, Bury Museum and Art Gallery, *Moss Street, www.bury.gov.uk 0161 253 5878.*
This refurbished museum and gallery is full of interactive games and activities enabling children to learn and have fun. Smell the sewers and meet the woolly mammoth. Events and fun days. Open Tues-Fri, 10am-5pm, Sat, 10am-4.30pm, Sun, 1-4pm. Schools **Open all year.**

Lancashire Fusiliers Museum, *Wellington Barracks, Bolton Road, www.fusiliersmuseum-lancashire.org.uk 0161 764 2208.*
A collection of Victoria Crosses helps to reflect the history of the regiment and its soldiers. See the gifts to the regiment from Napoleon, along with uniforms and personal artefacts. Open Tues-Sun, 10am-4pm. Schools **Open all year.**

ople's History Museum, *The Pump House, Bridge Street, www.peopleshistorymuseum.org.uk*
839 6061.
...ay your part' and dress up in this museum dedicated to the lives of ordinary people. Interactive displays, events programme and children's activities during school holidays. Open Tues-Sun and Bank Hol Mons, 11am-4.30pm. Schools **Open all year.**

Urbis, *Cathedral Gardens, www.urbis.org.uk 0161 907 9099.*
This state-of-the-art museum, set in a striking building, explores life in different cities around the world. Access is via the Glass Elevator Sky Glide. Many interactive displays - start at the top and work down. Open Tues-Sun, 10am-6pm. Schools Refreshments **Open all year.**

The Whitworth Art Gallery, *Oxford Road, Manchester, www.whitworth.manchester.ac.uk*
0161 275 7450.
See the popular 'textile tower' with art materials available; at weekends and in school holidays, try the art-cart with drawing materials and quizzes. Family events programme. Open Mon-Sat, 10am-5pm, Sun, 2-5pm. Schools Refreshments **Open all year.**

Norden, Three Owls Bird Sanctuary and Reserve, *Wolstenholme Fold, www.threeowls.co.uk*
01706 642162.
Relying heavily on donations, this sanctuary takes distressed wild birds, rehabilitates them and returns them to the wild. Between 400 and 1,500 birds can be seen. Open Suns, 12noon-4pm, (Mon-Fri 1-3pm by arrangement). Schools **Open all year.**

Oldham, Gallery Oldham, *Greaves Street, www.galleryoldham.org.uk 0161 911 4657.*
A mix of contemporary and traditional art together with exhibitions of local interest. Participate in hands-on events and activities during school holidays. Open Mon-Sat, 10am-5pm. Schools **Open all year.**

Prestwich, Heaton Hall and Heaton Park, *Middleton Road, www.manchester.gov.uk*
0161 773 1085.
Appreciate the beauty of this historic home. Park facilities include a boating lake, farm centre, animal centre, road train and tram museum. Park open daily; times and days vary for other activities. Hall open Apr-Oct, ring for further details. Schools Refreshments **Open all year.**

Reddish, Reddish Vale Country Park and Local Nature Reserve, *Mill Lane,*
www.stockport.gov.uk 0161 477 5637.
Discover a small farm and museum, butterfly conservation park and millponds. Follow the nature trail and look at displays in the visitor centre. Opening times vary for visitors centre. Schools **Open all year.**

Rochdale, Greater Manchester Fire Service Museum, *Maclure Road,*
www.manchesterfire.gov.uk 01706 901227.
As well as historical equipment, uniforms, models and photographs, there are re-creations of a Victorian street and a WWII blitz. Open to groups by appointment only. Ring for details. Schools **Open all year.**

Springfield Park, *Bolton Road, www.rochdale.gov.uk 01706 693075.*
Ride the miniature steam railway which runs most summer Sunday afternoons in this large traditional park with playground and sports facilities. **Open all year.**

Touchstones Rochdale, *The Esplanade, www.rochdale.gov.uk/touchstones 01706 864986.*
Hands-on exploration of the Egyptian display and activity tables in each of the galleries welcome children of all ages to learn and have fun. Events and workshops during school holidays. Open Mon-Fri, 10am-5.30pm, Sat-Sun and Bank Hols, 11am-4.30pm. Schools Refreshments **Open all year.**

sholme, Gallery of Costume, *Platt Hall, www.manchestergalleries.org 0161 224 5217.*
of the largest collections of clothing and accessories in Britain, with items dating from the
entury to the present day. Ideal for budding designers. Open last Sat of every month,
m. Schools **Open all year.**

Saddleworth, Brownhill Countryside Centre, *Wool Road, Dobcross, 01457 872598.*
Winner of a Green Flag Award. Learn all about the countryside with the nature garden, displays and exhibits. Younger children will love the woodland 'crawly' tunnel. Open Wed-Fri, 11am-4pm, Sat-Sun, 10.30am-5pm (4pm Nov-Mar). Schools Birthdays **Open all year.**

Huddersfield Narrow Canal Sculpture Trail, *from Ashton-under-Lyne to Huddersfield.*
The trail was designed by local artists and influenced by ideas from local schoolchildren. See unique works of art alongside the canal and enjoy the two themed play areas, both located in Diggle. **Open all year.**

Salford, Irwell Sculpture Trail, *along the River Irwell, 0161 253 5892.*
The largest public art scheme in the UK, starting at Salford Quays and extending to the West Pennine Moors. There are presently 28 sculptures to admire and events are organised throughout the year. **Open all year.**

The Lowry, *Salford Quays, www.thelowry.com 0870 787 5774.*
This stunning waterside location houses the largest public collection of L.S. Lowry's art, alongside changing exhibitions. There are family activities and events throughout the year and theatres with many children's performances. Gallery open Sun-Fri, 11am-5pm, Sat, 10am-5pm. Schools Refreshments **Open all year.**

Ordsall Hall, *Ordsall Lane, Ordsall, www.salford.gov.uk 0161 872 0251.*
Discover this furnished Tudor manor house in the heart of a busy housing estate. Family fun days on the first Sunday of the month and workshops, events and re-enactments throughout the year. Open Mon-Fri, 10am-4pm, Sun, 1-4pm. Schools **Open all year.**

Salford Museum and Art Gallery, *Peel Park, The Crescent, www.salford.gov.uk 0161 778 0800.*
Walk down the re-creation of a Victorian street with smells, sounds and dressing-up costumes The galleries display traditional and modern art with changing exhibitions. Children's activity sheets. Open Mon-Fri, 10am-4.45pm, Sat-Sun, 1-5pm. Schools Refreshments **Open all year.**

Stalybridge, Astley Cheetham Art Gallery, *Trinity Street, www.tameside.gov.uk 0161 338 6767.*
The gallery usually shows local work and artist materials for children are always available. Many and varied holiday activities, plus pre-bookable workshops. Open Mon-Wed & Fri, 10am-5pm, Sat, 9am-4pm; closed for lunch. **Open all year.**

Stockport, Hat Works, *Wellington Mill, Wellington Road South, www.hatworks.org.uk*
0845 833 0975.
If you have ever wondered how hats were made, then this is the place for you. Displays of hats throughout the ages include Indian headdresses, sportswear, emergency services headwear as well as some fanciful ladies creations both modern and historic. Try on some different styles and view the history of hat making from its origins as a cottage industry through to mechanisation in the mills. Family Fun Quiz sheets help you find your way around. Changing programme of exhibitions, storytelling and children's activities (charges may apply) throughout the year. Guided tours also available (price A). Open Mon-Fri, 10am-5pm, Sat-Sun & Bank Hol Mons, 1-5pm. Schools Birthdays Refreshments **Open all year Check out page 50.**

Stockport Art Gallery, *Wellington Road South/Greek Street, www.stockport.gov.uk 0161 474 4453.*
A traditional art gallery with children's Saturday Club and activities for families in school summer holidays. Open Mon-Tues and Thurs-Fri, 11am-5pm, Sat, 10am-5pm. Schools **Open all year.**

Stockport Museum, *Vernon Park, Turncoft Lane, Offerton, www.stockport.gov.uk 0161 474 4460.*
Learn about past and present with interactive displays and audiovisual shows. Trails and special events. The museum will be undergoing some refurbishment during 2006; please check before you visit. Open Mon-Fri, 10am-4pm, Sat-Sun, 1-5pm. Schools Refreshments **Open all year.**

Wigan, Haigh Country Park, *Haigh, www.haighhall.net 01942 832895.*
Ride the narrow-gauge railway and explore the play area. Make sure you visit the Stables Gallery with hands-on activities and demonstrations most days. Telephone for details of the events programme. Open daily, 9.30am-4.30pm. Schools Birthdays Refreshments **Open all year.**

Wythenshawe, Wythenshawe Hall and Park, *www.manchester.gov.uk 0161 998 2117.*
This historic house is furnished with original items from the Tatton family. The surrounding park contains a horticultural centre, woodland gardens and community farm. Park open daily, dawn-dusk; ring for Hall and farm opening times. Groups **Refreshments   Open all year**.

HISTORY, ART & SCIENCE

Altrincham, Dunham Massey, NT, *0161 941 1025.*
Stunning parkland with fallow deer and guided walks. Try the hands-on family tour of the mansion and explore life below stairs. See the restored water-powered sawmill. Special events. Deer park open daily. House, gardens and mill open Apr-Oct, days and times vary. Schools **Open all year Price B.**

Bolton, Bolton Wanderers FC Visitor & Tour Centre, *Reebok Stadium, Burden Way, www.bwfc.co.uk 01204 673670.*
An interactive museum tour centre looking at the club's history. See the managers' dug-outs, the dressing rooms and the media interview room. Open Mon-Fri, 9am-5pm, Sat, 9am-4pm, Sun, 11am-4pm. **Open all year Price A.**
Hall i'th' Wood, *Green Way, off Crompton Way, www.boltonmuseums.org.uk 01204 332370.*
Discover this historical home and learn all about life in Tudor and Stuart times. Dress up in Tudor costume and participate in the history trail. Special events and activities. Open Easter-Oct, Wed-Sun, 11am-5pm, Nov-Mar, Sat-Sun. Schools **Open all year Price A.**
Smithills Hall, *Smithills Dean Road, www.smithills.org 01204 332377.*
Set in restored gardens, this listed building with medieval connections has quiz sheets for children and events and activities during school holidays. Open summer, Tues-Sat, 11am-5pm, Sun, 2-5pm; winter, Tues & Sat, 1-5pm, Sun, 2-5pm. Schools **Open all year Price A.**

Bramhall, Bramall Hall, *Bramhall Park, www.bramallhall.org.uk 0161 485 3708.*
Explore the Victorian kitchen, servants' quarters and look out for mysterious priests' hides. Play area and events programme. Open Apr-Sept, Sun-Thurs, 1-5pm, Fri-Sat, 1-4pm, Bank Hols, 11am-5pm; winter opening times vary. Schools **Refreshments   Open all year   Price B.**

Disley, Lyme Park, NT, *01663 762023.*
Enjoy a tour of the house or a stroll in the deer park, featured in many film and TV productions. Play area and family events throughout the year. Park open daily. House and gardens, Easter-Oct, days and times vary. Schools **Refreshments   Open all year   Price B.**

Manchester, The Airport Tour Centre, *Terminal 1, Manchester Airport, www.tasmanchester.com 0161 489 2442.*
Tour a busy international airport. Find out what happens behind the scenes and try different jobs. Tours by prior appointment only. Schools **Refreshments   Open all year   Price B.**
Aviation Viewing Park, *Manchester Airport, www.manchesterairport.co.uk 0161 489 2442.*
Hear the roar as planes take off and land in front of you. A small visitors centre and a number of retired planes to get close to, including a Concorde (prices for Concorde tours 0161 489 3932).
Schools **Refreshments   Open all year   Price A.**
Manchester City Experience, *City Superstore, Reebok City, www.mcfc.co.uk 0870 062 1894.*
With videos of past glories, the club's heritage and tours of the stadium, players tunnel and dugouts, this is a must for any City fan. Open daily from 10am, phone to book. Groups
Refreshments   Open all year   Price C.
Manchester Jewish Museum, *190 Cheetham Hill Road, www.manchesterjewishmuseum.com 0161 834 9879.*
Learn about the Jewish community in Manchester and its history. Open Mon-Thurs, 10.30am-4pm, Sun, 10.30am-5pm. Schools **Open all year   Price A.**

Manchester United Museum and Tour Centre, *Sir Matt Busby Way, Old Trafford,*
www.manutd.com 0870 442 1994.
Follow the history of this famous club by going on a stadium tour and see the collection of memorabilia. Tours of the ground do not operate on match days. Open daily, 9.30am-5pm. Booking recommended. Schools Refreshments **Open all year** Price C.
Museum of Transport, *Boyle Street, Cheetham Hill, 0161 205 2122.*
Uncover the history of public transport, from a horse-drawn bus to Manchester's modern Metrolink. See the large collection of restored vehicles and a re-created workshop and ticket office. Open Wed, Sat-Sun and Bank Hols, 10am-5pm (4pm winter). Schools Refreshments **Open all year** Price A.

Rochdale, Ellenroad Engine House, *Elizabethan Way, Milnrow, www.ellenroad.org.uk*
01706 881952.
Explore the original 3,000-horsepower steam mill engines, saved and restored from a Lancashire cotton mill. Picnic area, special events and activities. Open Feb-Dec, first Sun of the month, 12noon-4pm. Schools Price A.
Rochdale Pioneers Museum, *Toad Lane, www.museum.co-op.ac.uk 01706 524920.*
Use the display, exhibition and re-created shop to learn about the co-operative retailing revolution and how the movement has evolved. Open Tues-Sat, 10am-4pm, Sun, 2-4pm. Schools **Open all year** Price A.

Many Museums have FREE entry. Check out the Free Places section.

Saddleworth, Saddleworth Museum and Art Gallery, *High Street, Uppermill,*
www.saddleworthmuseum.co.uk 01457 874093.
A small museum exploring local heritage, including a Roman fort. Hands-on activity area, family boxes and school holiday 'boredom busters'. Open Apr-Oct, Mon-Sat, 10am-4.45pm, Sun, 12noon-4.45pm; Nov-Mar, daily, 1-4.45pm. Schools Birthdays **Open all year** Price A.

Stockport, Staircase House, *Market Place, www.staircasehouse.org.uk 0161 480 1460.*
Staircase House is 'hands-on' in the most literal sense. There are no signs saying 'keep off' or 'do not touch', quite the opposite. You are positively encouraged to pull up a 200 year old chair at the dining table, or climb into the 17th century four poster bed in this 15th century merchant's house. Everything is out and accessible and it is all designed to give visitors the experience of how people lived in days gone by. An audio tour guides you through its 18 rooms, from 1460 to WWII, with activities along the way. Look out for the 'Stockport Story' museum opening 2006. Open daily, 1-5pm. Schools Refreshments **Open all year** Price A **Check out page 60.**
Stockport Air Raid Shelters, *Chestergate, www.stockport.gov.uk 0161 474 1940.*
Explore this labyrinth of purpose-built underground tunnels dug into the sandstone beneath Stockport. Experience wartime life. Guided tours available, please ring for details. Warm clothing and sensible shoes recommended. Open daily, 1-5pm. Schools **Open all year** Price B.

Wigan, The Wigan Pier Experience, *Wigan Pier, Trencherfield Mill, www.wiganpier.net*
01942 323666.
Ideal for families, Wigan Pier provides an educational and fun-packed day out, transporting visitors back in time to the Victorian period. History is brought to life by the Wigan Pier Theatre Company in 'The Way We Were'. Discover the strictness of the Victorian schoolroom and explore living conditions, including the outside loo. Imagine the ground shaking as you experience the Maypole Colliery Disaster. Watch the Trencherfield Mill Engine in action, and finish with a boat trip along the Leeds-Liverpool Canal. Special events throughout the year. Open Mon-Thurs, 10am-5pm, Sun, 11am-5pm. Schools **Open all year** V Price C **Check out page 60.**

BOAT TRIPS

Ashton-under-Lyne, Tameside Canal Boat Trust, *Portland Basin Museum, 0161 339 1332.*
The narrow boat 'Still Waters' takes you on a 40-minute trip along the Ashton Canal. Operates Easter-Oct, Sun, Bank Hols and, when possible, museum event days, 12noon-4pm. Always ring in advance to confirm trip operational. Groups **Price A.**

Littleborough, Hollingworth Lake, *www.rochdale.gov.uk 01706 370499.*
Try a 30-minute trip aboard the 'Lady Alice' motor launch. Operates Easter-Sept, Sat-Sun and school hols, from 12noon, weather permitting. **Price A.**

Saddleworth, Pennine Moonraker Canal Cruises, *Uppermill,*
www.saddleworth-canal-cruises.co.uk 0161 652 6331.
Enjoy an hour-long trip on a diesel-engine narrow boat along the Huddersfield Canal. Available for private charter. Operates hourly, Easter-mid Oct; Sat, 1-3pm, Sun, 12noon-4pm, Wed, 1-2pm, & daily in school hols. Schools Birthdays **Price A.**

BUS TRIPS

Manchester, City Sightseeing, *www.city-sightseeing.com 0871 666 0000.*
Hop on board an open-top bus for a tour of the city's attractions with running commentary and Kids Club activity pack. Operates May-Sept. **Price B.**
Stagecoach, *www.stagecoachbus.com/manchester*
Operating more than 100 services right across south Manchester including to and from Manchester city centre, Stockport, the Trafford Centre, Manchester Airport and many of the most popular day out destinations for children in the Greater Manchester area. Stagecoach offers flexible, value-for-money ticket options for adults travelling together with children; 'Groupdayrider' - one day's unlimited travel for up to 2 adults (over 16) and up to 3 children (under 16) at £5.60, and new for 2006 the 'Dayrider plus one' - one day's unlimited travel for one adult travelling with one child at £4.20. So why not leave the car at home and make the bus part of a fun day out together? Groups **Open all year Check out page 58.**

TRAIN TRIPS

Bury, East Lancashire Railway, *www.east-lancs-rly.co.uk 0161 764 7790.*
Journey back in time on the East Lancashire Railway and sample all the excitement of a steam train ride, passing over viaducts and through tunnels along the scenic Irwell Valley. Hop on board from Bury, Heywood, Rawtenstall or Ramsbottom or visit the riverside picnic area at Ramsbottom and wave as the trains go by. Celebrate over 60 years of Thomas and friends in May, August and October. Operates every weekend and Bank Hols throughout the year and Wed, Thurs & Fri, May-Sept. Price indicated is for a full line, return journey. Please call the Information Office 10am-4pm. Schools **Refreshments Open all year Price C Check out page 58.**

Dealing with asthma

In Association with
British Red Cross

Your son is having a birthday party and one of his invited friends suffers from asthma. Should she be prevented from taking part in the more physical party games?

No. It is safe for the friend to join in but it may be worth checking that she has an inhaler handy first.

To learn more about first aid visit redcross.org.uk/firstaid or call 0870 170 9222

www.letsgowiththechildren.co.uk

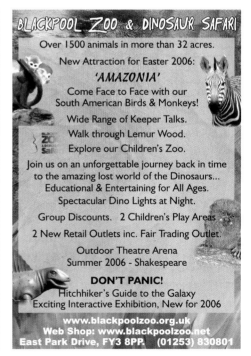

A mix of beautiful scenery and industrial heritage, Lancashire is perhaps best known for the cotton industry, which many museums in this area reflect. The Fylde coast offers many family destinations, the most famous being Blackpool, but there are also lots of places to explore off the beaten track. Many of the attractions in Blackpool have extended opening hours for the duration of the Illuminations.

ADVENTURE, FUN & SOFT PLAY

Blackburn, Waves Water Fun Centre, *Nab Lane, www.waveswaterfun.com 01254 51111.*
Whizz down the alien spacebowl water chute or try a gentle slide. Splash in the waves or relax in the jacuzzi. Opening times vary. Groups **Open all year** Price B.

Blackpool, Blackpool Model Village and Gardens, *East Park Drive, Stanley Park, www.blackpoolmodelvillage.com 01253 763827.*
Admire a miniature world set in beautiful gardens. A children's quiz sheet guides you through churches, cottages, bridges and a castle. A quiet alternative to the seafront attractions. Open daily, Apr-Nov, 10am-dusk. Groups Refreshments Price A.

Blackpool Tower & Circus, *www.theblackpooltower.com 01253 622242.*
A jaw-dropping 116 metres to the Tower Top Walk of Faith! Dare you look? Laugh at the antics in the Circus and enjoy Jungle Jim's enormous play area, the Aquarium and Dawn of Time ride. Opening times and prices vary. Groups Birthdays Refreshments **Open all year** Price E.

Louis Tussauds Waxworks, *Central Promenade, www.blackpoollive.com 01253 625953.*
Find over 200 waxworks and a display on how they are made. See stars from film, television, sport and royalty. Are you brave enough to enter the Chamber of Horrors? Please ring for opening times. Groups Refreshments **Open all year** Price B.

Pleasure Beach, *Ocean Boulevard, www.blackpoolpleasurebeach.co.uk 0870 444 5566.*
From white-knuckle rides to a special area for younger children, this is an attraction for all ages. Many rides are indoors. Free entry to the park, price applies to an unlimited ride ticket. Open Feb-Nov, times vary. Schools Birthdays Refreshments Price G.

Ripley's Believe It or Not, *Ocean Boulevard, www.ripleysblackpool.com 01253 341033.*
Travel around the world in seven themed galleries to discover the unusual, the bizarre and the unbelievable - tallest, smallest, fattest, thinnest. You can even see a million-dollar man. Open daily from 10am, closing times vary. Groups **Open all year** Price B.

Sandcastle Waterworld, *South Promenade, www.sandcastle-waterworld.co.uk 01253 343602.*
The Barracuda is one of the fastest flumes. Will you stand under the giant coconut when it empties or slow things down in the sleepy lagoon? New for 2006 is the 'Master Blaster' which slides uphill! Open Apr-Nov, daily from 10am, closing times vary. Groups Birthdays Refreshments Price C.

Chorley, Clown Around, *Grove Mill, The Green, Eccleston, www.anewwaytoplay.co.uk 01257 451600.*
Become a star for the day with the karaoke stage, or are you champion of the electronic dance mat? Celebrate your stardom on the slides, ball pools, and other play equipment. Open daily, 10am-4pm. Groups Birthdays Refreshments **Open all year** Price A.

Playmates, *Coppull Enterprise Centre, Mill Lane, 01257 470288.*
Discover a spooky hole, slides and bridges at this indoor adventure play centre. Keep-fit, music time and story time activities each week. Soft centre for under 5s. Open daily, 9.30am-4pm. Groups Birthdays Refreshments **Open all year** Price A.

Chorley(near), Camelot Theme Park, *Charnock Richard, www.camelotthemepark.co.uk 01257 452100.*
Dare you ride The Gauntlet or Whirlwind? Smaller children have lots of rides in Merlin's Playland. Daily jousting tournaments, Wizard School, Animal Kingdom and soft play area. Open Easter-Oct, from 10am, days and closing times vary. Schools Birthdays **Refreshments Price G.**

Heywood, Planet Play, *Bradshaw Street, www.planetplay.net 01706 627627.*
Aim the ball shooters at the targets in this three-storey, space-themed play barn. Continue the space theme in the dark room. Separate area for under 3s. Open daily, 10am-6.30pm. Groups Birthdays **Refreshments Open all year Price A.**

Horwich, Tumble Jungle, *Chorley New Road, 01204 696158.*
Aerial walkways, rope bridges and ball pools mean lots of excitement. Open daily, 10am-7pm. Groups Birthdays **Refreshments Open all year Price A.**

Morecambe, Megazone Laser Adventure, *The Megazone Building, Marine Road, www.megazonemorecambe.co.uk 01524 410224.*
A laser adventure full of excitement and fun. Open Mon-Fri, 12noon-10pm, Sat-Sun, 10am-10pm. Groups Birthdays **Refreshments Open all year Price P.**

Nelson, Pendle Wavelengths, *Leeds Road, www.pendleleisuretrust.co.uk 01282 661717.*
This is where it's always summertime! Brave the roof-high waterslide, jump above the waves or have fun in the beachside playland. Schools Birthdays **Refreshments Open all year Price A.**

Oswaldtwistle, Bubbles Play Centre, *Oswaldtwistle Mills, www.o-mills.co.uk 01254 770752.*
Squeeze between rollers, wade through ball pools and check out the slides at this indoor soft play centre. Separate areas for under 5s and babies. Open Mon-Sat, 9.30am-5pm, Sun, 10am-5pm. Groups Birthdays **Refreshments Open all year Price A.**

Preston, Cheeky Monkeys, *School Lane, Bamber Bridge, 01772 313133.*
Slither, slide and climb in the jungle-themed play area. Play team games in the sports court or join in the regular music, story or exercise activities. Open Mon-Sat, 9.30am-5.30pm, Sun, 10am-5.30pm. Groups Birthdays **Refreshments Open all year Price A.**

St Anne's, The Island, *South Promenade, www.the-island.ws*
This leisure park has a variety of activities, from boating lake to miniature railway, from swimming pool to ten-pin bowling. There are trampolines, a cinema, pitch and putt and the RNLI Visitors Centre. Opening times vary. **Refreshments Open all year Price P.**

FARMS, WILDLIFE & NATURE PARKS

Arkholme, Docker Park Farm Visitor Centre, *www.dockerparkfarm.co.uk 01524 221331.*
Visit Rabbit World where you can touch the rabbits and guinea pigs in their own little village. Feed the goats, meet the cows and hens then see the newly hatched chicks in spring. Also try your hand at feeding the spring lambs. Check out the horses from Clydesdale to Shetland and all sizes in between. Farm trail, indoor play barn and regular events. Open daily, Easter-Oct, 10.30am-5pm, Nov-Easter, Sat-Sun, 10.30am-4pm, and daily in school hols. Schools Birthdays **Refreshments Open all year V Price B Check out page 60.**

Blackpool, Blackpool Zoo, *East Park Drive, www.blackpoolzoo.org.uk 01253 830830.*
See over 1500 animals in 32 acres of mature lakes and parkland. Experience the Jurassic period in the Dinosaur safari. Coming in 2006, the chance to get up close to parrots and monkeys. Open daily from 10am, closing times vary. Schools Birthdays **Refreshments Open all year Price D Check out page 60.**
Sea Life Centre, *Golden Mile Promenade, www.sealifeeurope.com 01253 622445.*
Innovative displays of fish from around the world. Walk under sharks, come close to the serpents of the sea and discover the lost city of Atlantis. Daily feeding displays and indoor play area. Open daily from 10am, closing times vary. Schools Birthdays **Refreshments Open all year Price C.**

Burscough, Martin Mere Wildfowl and Wetlands Centre, *www.wwt.org.uk 01704 895181.*
Discover one of Britain's important wetland sites, home to birds and other wildlife. Events and activities programme during school holidays and a wetland adventure playground. Open daily, 9.30am-5.30pm (4.30pm Nov-Feb). Schools **Open all year** Price B.

Windmill Animal Farm, *Red Cat Lane, www.windmillanimalfarm.co.uk 01704 892282.*
See a wide variety of farm animals. Visit the pets corner and indoor and outdoor play areas, or take a train ride to the lake. Open daily, Easter-Sept, 10am-5pm, Oct-Easter, Sat-Sun & school hols. Schools Birthdays **Refreshments** Price B.

Carnforth, Leighton Moss Nature Reserve, RSPB, *Myers Farm, Silverdale, www.rspb.org.uk 01524 701601.*
Rare birds, common species and estuary wildlife inhabit the largest area of reedbed in the North West. Reserve open 9am-9pm or dusk if earlier. Visitor centre open daily, 9.30am-5pm (4.30pm Nov-Jan). Schools **Refreshments** **Open all year** Price A **Check out RSPB below and page 64.**

Chipping, Bowland Wild Boar Park, *www.wildboarpark.co.uk 01995 61554.*
A stunning location. See wild boar, deer, llamas, wallabies and more. There are four farm trails, tractor and trailer rides, lamb feeding from Easter to summer and a play and picnic area. Open daily, 10.30am-5.30pm. Schools Birthdays **Refreshments** **Open all year** Price B.

Fleetwood, Farmer Parrs Animal World, *Wyrefield Farm, Rossall Lane, www.farmerparrs.com 01253 874389.*
Get friendly with rare breed animals and feed the babies, or enjoy a pony or tractor ride. Indoor and outdoor play areas, pottery studio and large heritage centre. Open daily, 10am-5pm. Schools Birthdays **Refreshments** **Open all year** Price A.

Helmshore, Cronkshaw Fold Farm & Environmental Study Centre, *off Alden Road, 01706 218614.*
A traditional hill farm which focuses on sustainable farming. Public open days throughout the year with seasonal themed activities for children; telephone for further details. Schools Birthdays **Price A.**

Lancaster, Williamson Park, *www.williamsonpark.com 01524 33318.*
Enjoy the tropical atmosphere of the butterfly house, the mini-beast centre and small zoo, together with traditional park activities in the summer. Free entry to park; charges apply for butterfly house and mini-beast centre. Open daily, 10am-5pm (4pm Oct-Mar). Schools Birthdays **Refreshments** **Open all year** Price B.

Ormskirk, Farmer Ted's Farm Park, *Flatmans Lane, Downholland, www.farmerteds.com 0151 526 0002.*
Explore the straw mountain with its internal tunnels and slides. Alternatively, try a pedal tractor or play in the sandpit and playgrounds. Don't forget to visit the animals. Open Wed-Mon, 10am-6pm during school holidays. Check for other times. Schools Birthdays **Refreshments** Price B.

FREE PLACES

RSPB Wildlife Explorers, *www.rspb.org.uk/youth 01767 680551.*
Discover birds and explore wildlife with the Wildlife fun book, packed with fun facts and things to do. Find out about joining the RSPB Wildlife Explorers, a brilliant club where you can take part in activities, competitions, days out and much more. You'll receive a magazine every two months with all the latest news plus plenty of ways you can help make a difference. Hear about special events coming to your area and enter competitions to win great prizes. There are three magazines to suit different age groups – Wild Times for children under 8yrs with pictures, stories, puzzles and things to make and do, Bird Life for children 8yrs and over, packed with pictures, facts and competitions, and Wingbeat for members over 13yrs, written by other teenagers, tackling real wildlife issues. There are RSPB nature reserves all over the UK, some of which hold special events. Visit the website for more information. **Check out page 64.**

RSPB Wildlife Explorers

Send for your **free**
Wildlife fun book **TODAY**

FREE BOOKLET

just for you!

It's full of brilliant pictures, things to do and info about birds and other wildlife

RSPB Wildlife Explorers
is the junior membership of the Royal Society for the Protection of Birds

Fill out this form and return it to:
RSPB Wildlife Explorers, Free Booklet Offer, FREEPOST ANG 10850, 17 Birkheads Road, Reigate, RH2 9ZW

✂

Please rush me my FREE Wildlife fun book and information about RSPB Wildlife Explorers

First name

Surname

Date of birth
/   /

Boy Girl
Please tick one

Address

Postcode

I am a member of RSPB Wildlife Explorers Yes   No

If you are under 16, please ask your parent/guardian to read this.

We promise not to sell your details to anyone else. The RSPB would like to tell you about fun activities and things you can buy from us and RSPB Sales Ltd. The RSPB may review your details and use them for our market research and analysis. If you DO NOT want us to use your details in this way please tick

2NGWCP0109   Registered charity no 207076   460-2404-04-05

The Trough of Bowland, located in North East Lancashire, is an area of upland moor, formed from a meltwater channel at the end of the last period of glaciation. This peaceful area offers great walks and views dotted with small towns and villages.

Accrington, **Haworth Art Gallery,** *Haworth Park, Manchester Road, 01254 233782.*
Situated in lovely parkland, the gallery is home to a large collection of Tiffany glass. Art materials are available for children to use. Events, exhibitions and summer schools. Open Wed-Fri & Bank Hols, 2-5pm, Sat-Sun, 12noon-4.30pm. Schools **Open all year.**

Blackburn, **Blackburn Museum and Art Gallery,** *Museum Street, www.blackburn.gov.uk 01254 667130.*
View a changing programme of contemporary and community exhibitions with associated family and children's activities. Look out for Saturday and school holiday workshops. Open Tues-Sat, 10am-4.45pm. Schools **Open all year.**
Lewis Textile Museum, *Exchange Street, www.blackburn.gov.uk 01254 667130.*
Learn about the history of cotton production using hands-on activities and see the textile machinery used. Open Tues-Sat, 11am-4pm. Schools **Open all year.**
Witton Country Park and Visitor Centre, *Preston Old Road, www.blackburn.gov.uk 01254 55423.*
From parkland and woodland to farmland, this park has many facets. Stroll along the nature trails or take advantage of the cycleways and playground. Guided visits available for schools. Park open daily. Visitor centre open Apr-Sept, Mon-Sat, 1-4.30pm, Sun, 11am-4.30pm, Oct-Mar, Thurs-Sat & Sun. Schools Refreshments **Open all year.**

Blackpool is always a family favourite. The traditional centre of activity is the Golden Mile with its tram system, donkey rides, amusement arcades, funfairs, and many visitor attractions. There is the famous Blackpool Tower stretching overhead at one end and the Big One rollercoaster at the other, with the shoreline split by three piers. The Illuminations turn the promenade into a magical scene for young children. Why not see them from a horse-drawn buggy? But even in the daytime, Blackpool is the neon light capital of the north. Blackpool is flamboyant and shameless, with a heart of gold. It's not for the faint-hearted. For 2006 the Illuminations will run from 1st September until 5th November. There is a quieter side to Blackpool too. Just the other side of town you will find the Zoo, parks and a model village. Contact Blackpool Tourist Information Centre for more details (01253 478222).
Stanley Park, *West Park Drive, www.3piers.com*
Take a trip on the lake with boats for hire or picnic in the beautiful gardens. Playgrounds, trampolines, crazy golf, putting greens and sports pitches give lots of variety. Schools Refreshments **Open all year.**

Blackpool(near), **ILPH Penny Farm,** *Preston New Road, Peel, www.ilph.org 01253 766095.*
Dedicated to the rescue and rehabilitation of horses, this farm gives you a chance to see and meet the animals in its care. Information centre and guided tours available. Phone for details. Schools Refreshments **Open all year.**

Burnley, **Towneley Hall Art Gallery & Museum,** *Towneley Park, www.towneleyhall.org.uk 01282 424213.*
Visit this historic house, local craft museum and natural history centre with interactive activities – all located within the park. Special events programme. Open Sat–Thurs, 12noon-5pm. Schools Refreshments **Open all year.**
Weavers' Triangle Visitors Centre, *Burnley Wharf, 85 Manchester Road, www.weaverstriangle.co.uk 01282 452403.*
Take a trip back in time to discover life in a mill town. Discover what home was like in the Cellar Dwelling. Experience the re-created Victorian classroom and working model fairground. Open Easter-Sept, Sat-Tues, 2-4pm, Oct, Sun, 2-4pm. Schools Refreshments.

Chorley, Astley Hall Museum and Art Gallery, *Astley Park, www.chorley.gov.uk 01257 515927.* An Elizabethan building with a wealth of history. Free quizzes and rubbings. Ring for details of the events and activities programme. Open Apr-mid Sept, Sat-Sun, 12noon-5pm. Schools Refreshments.

Darwen, Darwen Jubilee Tower, *Beacon Hill, Darwen Moor, www.blackburn.gov.uk 01254 691239.*
A steep hill climb is rewarded with panoramic views from the top of this tower, built to honour Queen Victoria. On very clear days you can sometimes see the Welsh hills. **Open all year.**
Sunnyhurst Wood and Visitors Centre, *Earnsdale Road, www.blackburn.gov.uk 01254 701545.* Wander through 85 acres of woodland encompassing seven miles of footpaths, with circular walks beginning at just 10 minutes duration for little legs. The visitors centre houses information and activities. Phone for opening times. Refreshments **Open all year.**

Lancaster, Lancaster City Museum, *www.lancsmuseums.gov.uk 01524 64637.*
Investigate the history and archaeology of Lancaster and the surrounding area. Children can use clipboards and worksheets as learning tools. Exhibitions and events programme. Open Mon-Sat, 10am-5pm. Schools **Open all year.**
River Lune Millennium Park, *from Lancaster to Caton.*
Rich in birds and wildlife, this park has footpaths, cycleways and information stations. Take a walk and discover the works of art along the way. **Open all year.**

Leyland, Worden Park, *Runshaw Hall Lane, 01772 422316.*
This historic park includes an arts and crafts centre with a programme of workshops and activities. Try a trip on the miniature railway or a game of crazy golf (telephone for times). Open daily until dusk. Schools **Open all year.**

Lytham St Anne's, Ribble Discovery Centre, RSPB, *Fairhaven Lake, www.rspb.org.uk 01253 796292.*
Next to the Ribble estuary, the centre promotes an understanding of the area and its wildlife. Interactive displays, shop, mud sampling, guided walks and special events. Centre open daily, 10am-5pm. Schools **Open all year Check out page 64.**

Morecambe, Happy Mount Park, *Marine Road East, www.lancaster.gov.uk 01524 582836.*
Bulging with activities in summer particularly, this park has trampolines, golf, playgrounds and an indoor play area. Scheduled for summer 2006 is a new children's water play area with jets and fountains, so bring a towel. Open daylight hours. Schools Refreshments **Open all year.**
The Tern Project, *Morecambe Bay, www.tern.org.uk 01524 582808.*
This unique collection of artwork is situated along the promenade and includes the statue of Eric Morecambe. The art reflects the importance of the Bay as a home to wildfowl and wading birds. The stone jetty includes pavement games for all to enjoy. **Open all year.**

Oswaldtwistle, Oswaldtwistle Mills, *Colliers Street, www.o-mills.co.uk 01254 871025.*
A mill shop with textile museum, sweet factory and wildlife reserve. Adventure play area, nature walk and special events including fairground rides at weekends. Open Mon-Sat, 9.30am-5.30pm (Thurs 8pm), Sun, 11am-5pm. Groups Birthdays Refreshments **Open all year.**

Preston, Harris Museum and Art Gallery, *Market Square, www.harrismuseum.org.uk 01772 258248.*
Visit the 'Story of Preston' gallery to explore the city's history. Programme of exhibitions, contemporary art shows and family activities during some weekends and school holidays. Open Mon-Sat, 10am-5pm, Sun, 11am-4pm. Closed Bank Hols. Schools Refreshments **Open all year.**
The National Football Museum, *Preston North End FC, Sir Tom Finney Way, Deepdale, www.nationalfootballmuseum.com 01772 908442.*
Take part in a special edition of Match of the Day or try a penalty. Hands-on exhibitions charting the rise of the game. Open Tues-Sat, 10am-5pm, Sun, 11am-5pm; check match day opening times. Groups Refreshments **Open all year.**

Rossendale, Rossendale Museum, *Whitaker Park, Rawtenstall, www.lancsmuseums.gov.uk*
01706 244682.
Set in a picturesque park, the museum has an aviary, playground and picnic area. A natural history section features historic taxidermy and includes a young African elephant. Open Apr-Oct, Sat-Sun, Tues-Thurs, & Bank Hols, 1-4.30pm, Nov-Mar, 1-4pm. Schools **Open all year.**

Rufford, Mere Sands Wood, *Holmeswood Road, www.wildlifetrust.org.uk 01704 821809.*
Follow fully accessible footpaths through woodland and see pondlife, birdlife and wildflowers. Bird hides are available for public use. Visitor centre open daily, 9am-5pm. Schools **Open all year.**

Stannah, Wyre Estuary Country Park, *www.wyrebc.gov.uk 01253 857890.*
An important site for wildfowl and wading birds. Wild flowers, a variety of walking trails, a dedicated dog-free picnic area and ranger service. Park always open. Ecology Centre open daily, Apr-Oct, 10.30am-4.30pm, Nov-Mar, 11am-3pm. Schools Birthdays **Refreshments Open all year.**

HISTORY, ART & SCIENCE

Blackburn, Blackburn Rovers FC Ewood Ground Tours, *Ewood Park, www.rovers.com*
08701 123456.
Make an appointment with former Blackburn and England cap Ronnie Clayton to tour the grounds. Listen to a general commentary interspersed with personal anecdotes about the game from a player's perspective. By appointment only. Groups **Open all year** Price A.
Blackburn Town Centre Ghostwalks, *www.lancashirehillcountry.co.uk 01254 53277.*
Join your authentically dressed Victorian guide for an hour-long walking tour around Blackburn, discovering the heroes, villains, murders and hauntings of this old town. Operates 2nd Mon of the month by appointment. Groups **Price A.**

Blackpool, Doctor Who Exhibition, *Central Promenade, www.doctorwhoexhibitions.co.uk*
01253 299982.
'EXTERMINATE'. From Hartnell to Eccleston, this exhibition leads you from behind the sofa, through the TARDIS into displays of every kind. Find original costumes, scripts, photographs and enemies of every Doctor, including the infamous Daleks. Open daily, 10.30am-5.30pm. Groups **Price B.**

Burnley, Queen Street Textile Museum, *Harle Syke, www.yarns.lancashire.gov.uk 01282 412555.*
Investigate Victorian factory life and discover why weavers learned to lip-read and use sign language. Follow the activities of Mill Mouse. Special events programme. Open mid Mar-Nov; Mar & Nov, Tues-Thurs, 12noon-4pm, Apr & Oct, Tues-Fri, 12noon-5pm, May-Sept, Tues–Sat, 12noon-5pm, and all Bank Hol Suns & Mons. Schools **Price A.**
Rourkes Forge, *Vulcan Works, Accrington Road, www.rourkes.co.uk 01282 422841.*
This working forge produces elaborate ornamental gates and ironwork. It made the Paisley gates at Liverpool FC. Tours and demonstrations are available for pre-booked groups only. Open Mon-Fri, 8am-5pm. Groups **Refreshments Price B.**

Carnforth, Leighton Hall, *www.leightonhall.co.uk 01524 734474.*
This historic family home has a caterpillar maze and aviaries housing birds of prey. Flying displays each afternoon, weather permitting. Play area, woodland trail and events programme. Open May-Sept, Tues-Fri, Sun & Bank Hol Mons, 2-5pm (12.30-5pm in Aug). Schools **Refreshments Price B.**

Clitheroe, Clitheroe Castle Museum, *Castle Hill, www.ribblevalley.gov.uk 01200 424635.*
Try the exciting events programme during school holidays, which includes hands-on activities and workshops for all the family. Open Easter-Oct, Mon-Sat, 11.15am-4.30pm, Sun, 1-4.30pm; Nov-Easter, please ring for details. Schools **Price A.**

Fleetwood, Fleetwood Museum, *Queens Terrace, www.nettingthebay.org.uk 01253 876621.*
Follow the story of Fleetwood, from fishing and cargo port to holiday resort. Fishing quiz and a chance to become a virtual fisherman! Changing exhibitions throughout the season. Open Apr-Nov, Mon-Sat, 10am-4pm, Sun, 1-4pm. Schools **Refreshments Price A.**

Jacinta: Fleetwood's Heritage Trawler, *Fish Dock, Freeport, www.arcticcorsair.f9.co.uk 01253 878158.*
Imagine life aboard this 1972 Icelandic trawler. Take the guided tour by retired fishermen and see the bridge, galley and crew accommodation. Find out how people lived and worked on the sea in the fish room exhibition. Open daily, Easter-Oct, 10am-4pm. Schools **Price A.**

Helmshore, Helmshore Mills Textile Museums, *Holcombe Road, www.lancsmuseums.gov.uk 01706 226459.*
Family-friendly displays and hands-on activities tell the story of the textile industry. Follow the adventures of 'Cotton Cat' and use the activity trolleys to dress up or to learn about textures and fibres. Special events. Open Apr-Oct, Mon-Fri, 12noon-4pm, Sat-Sun, 12noon-5pm. Schools **Refreshments Price A.**

Hoghton, Hoghton Tower, *www.hoghtontower.co.uk 01254 852986.*
A 16th century manor house with connections to William Shakespeare and the naming of beef 'Sirloin'. See underground passages, dungeons and gardens. Events programme. Open Jul-Sept, Mon-Thurs, 11am-4pm, Sun, 1-5pm, and some Bank Hols, ring for details. Schools **Refreshments Price B.**

Lancaster, Cottage Museum, *Castle Hill, www.lancsmuseums.gov.uk 01524 64637.*
This small museum is an artisan's house with low ceilings and narrow stairs. It dates from 1739 and is furnished as in Victorian times. Open daily, Easter-end Sept, 2-5pm. Schools **Price A.**

Judges' Lodgings, *Church Street, www.lancsmuseums.gov.uk 01524 32808.*
Play some period games in the handling room whilst visiting this Museum of Childhood. See the re-created playroom and Victorian schoolroom and an exhibition of dolls and toys from the 18th century to the present day. Events programme. Open Easter-Oct, times vary. Schools **Refreshments Price A.**

Lancaster Castle, *Castle Hill, www.lancastercastle.com 01524 64998.*
Be on your best behaviour. You will visit the Grand Jury Room, the Crown Court and the Dungeons. If you had been found guilty in times past, you might have been deported to Australia or hanged from the gallows. Guided tours only. Open daily, 10am-5pm. Schools **Open all year Price B.**

Maritime Museum, *Custom House, St George's Quay, www.lancsmuseums.gov.uk 01524 64637.*
Relish the sounds and smells of the past as you learn about the port of Lancaster's fishing industry and about Morecambe Bay and its ecology. Open daily, Easter-Oct, 11am-5pm, Nov-Easter, 12.30-4pm. Schools **Refreshments Open all year Price A.**

Leyland, British Commercial Vehicle Museum, *King Street, www.commercialvehiclemuseum.co.uk 01772 451011.*
Visit the largest commercial vehicle museum in Europe, home to historic vans, trucks and buses. Events throughout the season. Open Apr-Sept, Sun, Tues-Thurs and Bank Hol Mons, 10am-5pm, Oct, Suns only. Schools **Refreshments Price A.**

Nelson(near), Pendle Heritage Centre, *Park Hill, Barrowford, www.htnw.co.uk 01282 661702.*
Learn about the history of the house and follow the story of the Pendle witches. Animal barn and walled garden, art gallery and museum. Open daily, 10am-5pm. Schools **Refreshments Open all year Price A.**

Padiham, Gawthorpe Hall, *NT, 01282 771004.*
A stately home noted for its interior and textile collection. Follow the I-spy trail and take a riverside or woodland walk. Events programme. Gardens open daily, 10am-6pm. Hall open Easter-Oct, Tues-Thurs, Sat-Sun and Bank Hols, 1-5pm. Schools **Refreshments Open all year Price A.**

Preston, Guided Tours. Discover Preston's past by following one of the many 'spotlight tours' which take place Apr-Oct. Contact Tourist Information for details on 01772 253731.
The Museum of Lancashire, *Stanley Street, www.lancsmuseums.gov.uk 01772 264075.*
Discover the Victorian schoolroom, enjoy a tour through the Home Front during WWII and move on to the Fifties. This museum charts the history of the county and has three regimental galleries. Open Mon-Wed & Fri-Sat, 10.30am-5pm. Schools **Open all year** Price A.

Ribchester, Ribchester Roman Museum, *Riverside, www.ribchestermuseum.org 01254 878261.*
This museum is dedicated to the history of Bremetenacum Veteranorum, now known as Ribchester. See the artefacts in the museum or look around the remains of the fort. Open Mon-Fri, 10am-5pm, Sat-Sun, 12noon-5pm. Schools **Open all year** Price A.

Rufford, Rufford Old Hall, NT, *01704 821254.*
A 16th century building famous for its spectacular Great Hall. Rufford's Meadow is a lovely place to picnic and play. Quiz sheets and toys for the very young in the sitting room. Special events programme. Open 25th Mar-end Oct, Sat-Wed. Grounds, 11am-5pm. House, 1-5pm. Schools **Price B.**

Thornton-Cleveleys, Marsh Mill Windmill, *Fleetwod Road North, www.wyrebc.gov.uk 01253 860765.*
Take a guided tour to the very top of this restored windmill dating from 1794. There is an exhibition of milling and frequent demonstrations and workshops. Open Easter-Oct, Sat-Sun & Bank Hols, 10.30am-4.30pm, Nov-Easter, 11am-3pm. Schools **Open all year** Price A.

Turton, Turton Tower, *Chapeltown Road, www.lancsmuseums.gov.uk 01204 852203.*
Explore this country home where period rooms re-create history. A 'Billy Badger' pack includes a woodland discovery trail and indoor mystery tour. Events programme with family activities. Telephone for opening times. Schools **Refreshments** Price A.

TRIPS & TRANSPORT

BUS TRIPS

Blackpool, City Sightseeing, *www.city-sightseeing.com 0871 666 0000.*
Hop on board an open-top bus for a tour of the town's attractions with running commentary and Kids Club activity pack. Operates May-Sept. **Price B.**

TRAIN TRIPS

Blackpool, DalesRail, *www.dalesrail.com 01200 429832.*
This special leisure service runs from Blackpool to Carlisle and offers a scenic train journey together with organised walks - the easy walk is the most suitable for younger children. Operates Easter-Oct, Suns only. Please telephone for details. Schools.

Preston(near), West Lancashire Light Railway, *Station Road, Hesketh Bank, www.westlancs.org 01772 815881.*
One of the restored ex-industrial locomotives takes you on a short ride along this narrow-gauge steam railway. Special events during summer and 'Santa Specials' in Dec. Open Easter-Oct, Suns and Bank Hols. Schools Birthdays **Price A.**

TRAM TRIPS

Blackpool, Blackpool Tramway System, *www.blackpooltransport.com 01253 473000.*
Take a trip on the first electric tramway in Britain. Some of the vehicles still in use today are more than 100 years old. Special tours during Blackpool Illuminations in highly decorated trams. Frequent daily service. Groups **Open all year** Price P.

Merseyside

Perhaps best known for the music industry, Merseyside offers a diverse range of attractions, from sandy beaches and rural villages to busy inner city life. Many family-friendly activities are centred in Liverpool, awarded Capital of Culture status for 2008. Hundreds of years of history, including the slave trade, are attached to the famous River Mersey.

ADVENTURE, FUN & SOFT PLAY

Aintree, Time Out, *Heysham Road, www.timeoutchildrensplaycentre.co.uk 0151 525 3353.*
Ride a banana or have a game of football or basketball. A large indoor soft play centre with ball pools, gliders and slides. Open daily, 10am-7pm. Groups Birthdays **Refreshments Open all year** Price A.

Bebington, Madhouse, *Bebington Road, www.madhousesoftplay.co.uk 0151 644 5111.*
A soft play area with a house theme. Slides, ball ponds, climbing equipment and much more. Open Mon-Fri, 10am-5pm, Sat-Sun, 10am-4pm. Groups Birthdays **Refreshments Open all year** Price A.

Birkenhead, Europa Pools, *Conway Street, www.wirral.gov.uk 0151 647 4182.*
Splash down the flumes or relax in the jacuzzi. Enjoy the children's lagoon and a wave machine every 30 minutes. Open Mon-Fri, 3.30-8pm, Sat-Sun, 9.30am-6pm. Times are for all flumes and waves; phone for additional opening times. Schools Birthdays **Refreshments Open all year** Price B.

Brimstage, Maize Maze, *Brimstage Hall, www.icep.org.uk 07709 339490.*
Explore this maize maze with puzzles and quizzes to occupy you on the way round. Open Jul-Sept, please telephone for times. Groups **Price B.**

Liverpool, Happy Dayz, *Townsend Lane, 0151 256 6663.*
Plenty of scope for soft play fun at this Disney-themed indoor play centre with special area for under 5s. Groups Birthdays **Refreshments Open all year** Price A.

New Brighton, The New Palace, *Marine Promenade, 0151 639 6041.*
Adventureland indoor play includes a 7m climbing wall, trampolines and high slides along with toddler areas. There is an outdoor funfair and indoor amusement arcade. Open Sat-Sun & school hols, 11am-5pm. Groups Birthdays **Refreshments Open all year** Price P.

Seacombe, Play Planet, *Seacombe Ferry Terminal, www.merseyferries.co.uk 0151 330 1444.*
Three floors of space-themed fun within the ferry terminal, including a 'black hole', an 'asteroid belt' and space pods to wave from. Open daily, 10am-5pm. Groups Birthdays **Refreshments Open all year** Price A.

Southport, Lakeside Miniature Railway, *Marine Lake, www.lakesideminiaturerailway.co.uk 01772 745511.*
Take a trip alongside the lake and down to the beach on this miniature railway, which has been operating since 1911. Open daily, Easter-end Oct, weather permitting. Schools **Price A.**
Pleasureland, *Marine Drive, www.pleasureland.uk.com 0870 200 0204.*
Over 100 rides and attractions, including the Traumatizer and Chaos roller coasters and special junior area for younger children. Open Mar-Nov, days and times vary, phone for details and prices. Schools Birthdays **Refreshments Price P.**
Silcock's Funland, *Southport Pier, www.silcock-leisure.co.uk 01704 536733.*
A large indoor family amusement centre. There are slot machines, arcade and video games and a mini-ride for younger children. Open daily, times vary. Groups **Refreshments Open all year** Price P.

Southport Model Railway Village, *Lower Promenade, Kings Gardens,*
www.southportmodelrailwayvillage.co.uk 01704 538001.
Follow the miniature trains around 500m of track laid within the rural and urban settings of this model village. All set in 15 acres of landscaped gardens. Open daily, Easter-end Oct, 10am-5pm.
Schools **Refreshments Price A.**

Turbo Ted's Play Centre, *Princes Street, 01704 530165.*
Indoor adventure for under 5s includes soft play, trampolines, ball pool, slides and trikes.
Birthdays **Refreshments Open all year Price A.**

FARMS, WILDLIFE & NATURE PARKS

Brimstage, Brimstage Family Farm, *Brimstage Hall, www.icep.org.uk 0151 342 1725.*
This small family farm allows children to meet the animals and use the play area. It is set within the Brimstage Hall complex, which offers craft shopping and occasional activities. Open daily, summer, 10.30am-5pm, winter, 11am-4pm. Schools Birthdays **Refreshments Open all year Price A.**

Kirkby, Acorn Venture Farm, *Depot Road, www.acornfarm.co.uk 0151 548 1524.*
Goat-milking demonstrations and pony rides at weekends and in school holidays allow children to get close to the animals. Woodland walk, play area, activities and shop with home-grown produce. Open daily, 10am-4pm. Schools Birthdays **Refreshments Open all year Price A.**

Knowsley, Knowsley Safari Park, *Prescot, www.knowsley.com 0151 430 9009.*
Drive up close to lions, elephants, bison and zebra, but the cheeky baboons are most children's favourite. There is also a farm, amusement rides, parrot show and bug house. Open daily, Mar-Oct, 10am-4pm, Nov-Feb, 11am-3pm. Schools Birthdays **Refreshments Open all year Price C.**

Liverpool, National Wildflower Centre, *Court Hey Park, Roby Road, www.nwc.org.uk*
0151 738 1913.
See delightful wildflowers grown in an environmentally friendly way and get some ideas to try at home. Visit the small tree house play area or live like a bee in the beehive. Special events. Open daily, Apr-Sept, 10am-5pm. Schools **Refreshments Price A.**

Neston, Ness Botanic Gardens, *South Wirral, www.nessgardens.org.uk 0151 353 0123.*
Renowned gardens with walking trails, children's adventure playground and picnic area. New visitors centre planned for 2006. Open daily, Mar-Oct, 9.30am-5pm, Nov-Feb, 9.30am-4pm.
Schools **Refreshments Open all year Price A.**

Seacombe, Seacombe Aquarium, *Seacombe Ferry Terminal, Victoria Place, 0151 330 1444.*
Use the interactive displays to learn all about the marine life of the River Mersey at this small aquarium, which is home to baby sharks, a blushing octopus and a conger eel. Open daily, 10am-6pm. Schools Birthdays **Open all year Price A.**

FREE PLACES

Bidston, Tam O'Shanter Urban Farm, *Boundary Road, www.tamoshanterfarm.org.uk*
0151 653 9332.
Feed the hens on this traditional farm, home to pigs, goats, donkeys and more. Spend time with the animals and in the workshops, then walk up Bidston hill to see its windmill. Open daily, 9.30am-4.30pm. Schools Birthdays Refreshments **Open all year.**

Birkenhead, Birkenhead Priory & St Mary's Tower, *Priory Street, www.wirral.gov.uk*
0151 666 1249.
Nestled amongst Cammell Laird's cranes, this monastic ruin is the oldest standing building on Merseyside (1150). Climb the tower for magnificent views across the Mersey. Open summer, Wed-Sun, 10am-5pm, winter, Sat-Sun, 10am-4pm. Schools **Open all year.**

Shore Road Pumping Station, *Hamilton Street, www.wirral.gov.uk 0151 650 1182 or 0151 666 4010.*
See the 'Giant Grasshopper', used to clear water during the construction of the Mersey railway tunnel, and a 1901 Birkenhead street scene. Open summer, Sat-Sun, 1-5pm, winter, 12noon-4pm; also school hols & at some other times. Schools **Open all year.**
Wirral Museum, *Hamilton Square, www.wirral.gov.uk 0161 666 4010.*
Small exhibits detailing the history of the area, Cammell Laird shipyard and the ships built there. The museum is housed in the old Town Hall, built with typical Victorian splendour. Open Tues-Sun & Bank Hol Mons, 10am-5pm. Schools **Open all year.**

Formby, Formby Squirrel & Nature Reserve, NT, *Freshfield, 01704 878591.*
Feed the red squirrels, follow one of the walks or join in an event from the activity programme. The beach is part of one of the largest sand dune systems in England. Open daily from 9am. Schools **Open all year.**

Liverpool, Albert Dock, *www.albertdock.com 0151 708 7334.*
This restored Victorian dock is the largest group of Grade I listed buildings in Great Britain. Enjoy a lively mix of museums, galleries, shops, bars and cafés, together with temporary exhibitions, events and entertainment. The Albert Dock is also home of the Annual Mersey River Festival, a four-day event which includes tall ships, street theatre, music and displays.
Anglican Cathedral, *Hope Street, www.liverpoolcathedral.org.uk 0151 709 6271.*
Climb the tower of the largest cathedral in Britain (charges apply). There are events, activities, exhibitions and children's quizzes throughout the year. Cathedral open daily, 8am-6pm. Tower open Sats, 11am-5pm. Schools Refreshments **Open all year.**
Calderstones Park, *Menlove Avenue, www.liverpool.gov.uk 0151 225 4826.*
A Green Flag Award-winning park with a large lake, the remains of an ancient burial ground (the Calderstones), tennis courts and playground. Can you find the 1,000-year-old Allerton Oak? Groups Refreshments **Open all year.**
Conservation Centre, *Whitechapel, www.liverpoolmuseums.org.uk 0151 478 4999.*
The museum showing how our historical artefacts are cared for is being redeveloped. The new interactive exhibition space and working laboratory are scheduled to re-open in spring 2006. Please ring for details before visiting.
H M Customs and Excise National Museum, *Merseyside Maritime Museum, Albert Dock, www.liverpoolmuseums.org.uk 0151 478 4499.*
Learn about the battle against smuggling over the years. Interactive displays include identifying the smuggler! Special events all year. Open daily, 10am-5pm. Schools Refreshments **Open all year.**
Merseyside Maritime Museum, *Albert Dock, www.liverpoolmuseums.org.uk 0151 478 4499.*
Find out about Liverpool's connection with the slave trade. Learn about life as a merchant seaman during WWII. See the street scenes or take part in the family activities. Open daily, 10am-5pm. Schools Refreshments **Open all year.**
Museum of Liverpool Life, *Pier Head, www.liverpoolmuseums.org.uk 0151 478 4080.*
Appear on TV with the cast of Brookside, or view swimwear from yesteryear. This museum explores the social history of Liverpool, from the diverse cultures and communities to housing and health. Family events and activities. Open daily, 10am-5pm. Schools **Open all year.**
Rice Lane City Farm, *Walton Park Cemetery, Rawcliffe Road, 0151 530 1066.*
Pigs, sheep, cattle, goats, ponies and poultry live on this rare breeds farm of 24 acres. Guided walks and tours are available. Donations welcome. Open daily, 9am-4pm. Schools Refreshments **Open all year.**
Sefton Park and Sefton Park Palm House, *www.palmhouse.org.uk 0151 726 2415.*
The largest park in Liverpool is home to the restored Palm House, which is open daily, though times vary (see website for details). A great park for picnics and exploring. Schools Refreshments **Open all year.**

Tate Liverpool, *Albert Dock, www.tate.org.uk 0151 702 7400.*
See displays of modern and contemporary art. Drop-in activities on Sunday afternoons and special children's workshops last Sunday every month (phone for details). Games and children's trails. Gallery open Tues-Sun, 10am-5.50pm. Schools **Refreshments Open all year.**

The Walker, *William Brown Street, www.thewalker.org.uk 0151 478 4199.*
Become an art detective with a number of quiz sheets, or draw in the children's activity room. Art displays are classical and contemporary with changing exhibitions. Open daily, 10am-5pm. Schools **Refreshments Open all year.**

World Museum Liverpool, *William Brown Street, 0151 478 4399.*
Five floors house an aquarium, bug house, dinosaurs and planetarium. The Clore Natural History Centre and the Weston Discovery Centre are full of hands-on activities, crafts and puzzles. Open daily, 10am-5pm. Schools **Refreshments Open all year.**

Port Sunlight, Lady Lever Art Gallery, *www.ladyleverartgallery.org.uk 0151 478 4136.*
A traditional gallery and home to a collection of paintings and sculpture. Family packs and quizzes are available. Open daily, 10am-5pm. Schools **Refreshments Open all year.**

Prescot, Prescot Museum, *Church Street, www.knowsley.gov.uk 0151 430 7787.*
Visit the 'time' room with costumes to try on, time-related interactive exhibits and activity trail. Local history display and changing temporary exhibits. Special events with workshops in school holidays. Open Tues-Sat, 10am-1pm & 2-5pm, Sun, 2-5pm. Schools **Open all year.**

Southport, Atkinson Art Gallery, *Lord Street, www.atkinsonfriends.org.uk 0151 934 2110.*
A traditional gallery with colouring sheets and crayons available for children. Family activities and workshops in school holidays. Open Mon-Tues, Wed & Fri, 10am-5pm, Thurs & Sat, 10am-1pm. Closed Bank Hols. Schools **Open all year.**

Southport Botanic Gardens, *Churchtown, www.southport.gb.com 01704 228535.*
Beautiful gardens, fresh air and lots of activities, such as a boating lake, crazy golf, playground, aviary and small museum. Gardens open daily, 8am-dusk. Groups **Refreshments Open all year.**

Thurstaston, Royden Park, *Frankby, www.wirral.gov.uk 0151 677 7594.*
Explore acres of woodlands which lead up to Thurstaston Common and its sandstone outcrops. A miniature railway operates most Sundays. **Open all year.**

Wirral Coastline runs from Seacombe Ferry to West Kirby. Admire sculptures and the Liverpool waterfront when walking this coastal path. It is, on the whole, flat and car-free, making it ideal for cycling. The beaches of Wallasey, Meols and West Kirby received awards for water quality in 2005. There are sand dunes and many opportunities for watersports along the way. At low tide you can walk from West Kirby to Hilbre Island Nature Reserve in the mouth of the Dee estuary.

Wirral, Wirral Country Park, *Station Road, www.wirral.gov.uk*
Following an old railway line, this park has 12 miles of footpaths, with shorter pathways into other areas and great views over the Dee estuary to North Wales. Visitor Centre and guided walks. Visitor Centre open daily, 10am-5pm. Schools **Open all year.**

HISTORY, ART & SCIENCE

Aintree, The Grand National Experience, *Aintree Racecourse, Ormskirk Road, www.aintree.co.uk 0151 523 2600.*
Dress as a jockey in the weighing room or have a go on the computerised race. The visitor centre also includes a museum and racecourse tours are available (must be pre-booked). Ring for opening times. Groups **Refreshments Open all year** Price B.

Birkenhead, Historic Warships, *East Float Dock, Dock Road, www.historicwarships.org* *0151 650 1573.*
Climb onboard and explore two Falklands War ships and a minehunter. Visitor centre with interactive displays and models. Open daily, summer, 10am-5pm, winter, 10am-4pm; Jan-Feb, weekends only. Schools **Refreshments Open all year** Price B.

Liverpool, The Beatles Story, *Britannia Vaults, Albert Dock, www.beatlesstory.com 0151 709 1963.* This popular museum charts the sensational rise to fame of the Fab Four. Audio tour, children's activity pack with puzzles and games, and special events. Open daily, 10am-6pm. Schools **Open all year** Price C.

Croxteth Hall & Country Park, *Muirhead Avenue East, www.croxteth.co.uk 0151 228 5311.*
An Edwardian mansion with beautiful walled garden and working rare breeds farm. The country park has an adventure playground and special events throughout the year. Park open daily, until dusk. Hall, farm and gardens, summer, 10.30am-5pm. Farm only, winter, Sat-Sun, 11am-4pm. Schools Birthdays **Refreshments Open all year** Price B.

Everton Stadium Tour, *Goodison Park, www.evertonfc.com 0151 330 2305.*
Tour the home of the blue side of Liverpool. Visit the trophy room and dug-outs before seeing where Rooney and Lineker once sat in the changing rooms. Pre-booking essential. Groups Birthdays **Price B.**

Liverpool Football Club Museum and Tour Centre, *Anfield Road, www.liverpoolfc.tv* *0151 260 6677.*
Discover the club's history with archive footage, trophies and memorabilia in the museum and then tour the ground. Fans can walk down the tunnel and visit the changing rooms and dug-outs. Booking essential. Open daily, 10am-4pm. Schools **Open all year** Price C.

The Slavery History Trail, *0151 726 0941 or 0151 709 7682.*
This guided walking tour departs from the Merseyside Maritime Museum. Learn about Liverpool's connection with slavery. Operates Sat-Sun, 11am, or by prior booking throughout the week. Groups **Open all year** Price A.

Western Approaches, *Rumford Street, www.liverpoolwarmuseum.co.uk 0151 227 2008.*
Originally command headquarters for the Battle of the Atlantic. Try on a gas mask for size in this underground labyrinth of corridors. There is also an exhibition of wartime life. Open Mar-Oct, Mon-Thurs & Sat, 10.30am-4.30pm. Schools **Price B.**

Williamson Tunnels Heritage Centre, *The Old Stableyard, Smithdown Lane,* *www.williamsontunnels.co.uk 0151 709 6868.*
Unearth the myths which explain why a system of tunnels, leading nowhere, exists beneath the streets of Liverpool. Spend time in the heritage centre before taking the tour. Open summer, Tues-Sun & Bank Hol Mons, 10am-6pm; winter, Thurs-Sun, 10am-5pm. Additional opening Feb & Oct half terms. Schools **Refreshments Open all year** Price A.

Port Sunlight, Port Sunlight Heritage Centre, *Greendale Road, www.portsunlightvillage.com* *0151 644 6466.*
The centre is currently undergoing major renovation and is scheduled to re-open in summer 2006. Ring for details before visiting.

St Helens, The World of Glass, *Chalon Way East, www.worldofglass.com 0870 011 4466.*
Explore the tunnels of the Victorian glass furnace. Watch glass blowing demonstrations or experiment in Glass Magic to find the illusions glass can create. Open Tues-Sun & Bank Hol Mons, 10am-5pm. Schools **Refreshments Open all year** Price B.

Seacombe, Spaceport, *Seacombe Ferry Terminal, www.spaceport.org.uk 0151 330 1333.*
Fly in the Space Explorer Craft or get interactive on a virtual tour through space, from Earth to the far reaches of the universe. For more information see Mersey Ferries in 'Trips' section. Open Tues-Sun, 10.30am-5.30pm, Bank Hol Mons, and throughout Aug. Schools **Refreshments Open all year** Price B.

Speke, Speke Hall, NT, *signposted from Liverpool Airport, 0151 427 7231.*
The half-timbered mansion boasts a priest-hole and 'thunderbox' toilet. Children's activity packs and costumed tours are available. Gardens and playground open daily, 11am-5.30pm (dusk in winter). Hall open Mar-Oct, Wed-Sun, 1-5.30pm, Nov-Dec, Sat-Sun, 1-4.30pm. Schools Refreshments **Open all year Price B.**

BOAT TRIPS

Liverpool, Mersey Ferries, *River Explorer Cruises, Pier Head www.merseyferries.co.uk*
0151 330 1444.
Family cruises on the River Mersey with commentary telling the story of Liverpool's historic past. There is a free children's activity pack with child return Explorer tickets. This trip allows you to break your journey by stopping at Seacombe and Woodside Terminals and to rejoin and complete your cruise later that day. Buy a joint ticket to visit Spaceport at Seacombe and experience a virtual journey through space. Become an astronaut on an exploration of our solar system in the 180 degree Space Dome immersive cinema show, then fly through space in the Space Explorer Craft. See real Starchaser rockets that have recently flown from Britain's space programme and experiment with lots of hands-on interactive displays. Also visit the aquarium where you can learn about the underwater world of the River Mersey, try Play Planet soft play area for 2-9 year olds whilst you relax in the café, or enjoy a walk along the promenade to New Brighton. At Woodside, why not stop for lunch or afternoon tea at the café and visit Birkenhead Priory or the Wirral Museum? Operates Mon-Fri, 10am-3pm, Sat-Sun, 10am-6pm. Schools Birthdays Refreshments **Open all year Price B/C Check out inside front cover.**
Yellow Duck Marine, *Anchor Courtyard, Albert Dock, www.theyellowduckmarine.co.uk 0151 708 7799.*
Try this WWII amphibious landing vehicle which starts on dry land touring the major sights of Liverpool's city centre. Then splash down into the Salthouse Dock for a unique experience. Trips run daily, summer departures, 11am-5.15pm, winter, 11am-4.15pm. Schools Birthdays **Price D.**

Southport, Marine Lake, *www.visitliverpool.com 01704 539701.*
Two very different boat trips: a gentle cruise aboard the 'Southport Belle' with a commentary or an exciting high-speed ride aboard the 'Southport Jetboat'. Trips operate Easter-Jun & Sept, Sat-Sun; Jul-Aug, daily sailings. **Price P.**

BUS TRIPS

Liverpool, City Sightseeing, *www.city-sightseeing.com 0871 666 0000.*
Hop on board an open-top bus for a tour of the city's attractions with running commentary and Kids Club activity pack. Operates Mar-Oct. **Price B.**

Wirral, City Sightseeing, *www.city-sightseeing.com 0871 666 0000.*
As above. Operates Jul-Sept. **Price B.**

TRAM TRIPS

Birkenhead, Birkenhead Tramway, *Wirral Transport Museum, 1 Taylor Street,*
www.wirraltransportmuseum.org 0151 647 2128.
Ride the Victorian tram from Woodside Ferry to the Museum and then climb aboard many more vehicles. There is also a model train layout. Operates Sat-Sun, summer, 1-5pm, winter, 12noon-4pm. Additional opening in summer school hols. Schools **Open all year Price A.**

www.letsgowiththechildren.co.uk

Get an EXTRA Day and Night FREE!

© Disney

'Let's Go With The Children' customers are invited to take advantage of this fantastic special offer and take a truly magical 2, 3 or 4 night break to *Disneyland*® Resort Paris and **get an extra night** including breakfast in your Disney Hotel, **plus an extra day** to explore both Disney Parks – **absolutely free!**

So that's more time to experience all the high speed thrills, amazing attractions and magical Disney moments.

For arrivals 6–13 March, 17–21 April 17–21 May, 12–16 June, 13–17 September and 4–7 October 2006 inclusive, you will receive:

✦ **3 nights/4 days**
for the price of 2 nights/3 days

✦ **4 nights/5 days**
for the price of 3 nights/4 days

✦ **5 nights/6 days**
for the price of 4 nights/5 days

For further information or to book, call
08705 03 03 02
and quote code DSA.
Visit **www.disneylandparis.com**

*See website for full terms & conditions.

Great Family Breaks

Looking for a holiday or break that really caters for families? We've talked to some of the key family specialist operators and here is what they are offering in 2006.

Chilly Powder, *www.chillypowder.com 0207 289 6958.*
If you are looking for a summer break in France, try Chilly Powder who have chalets in Morzine, an appealing Savoyarde village near the French/Swiss border. Chilly Powder provides facilities and equipment for children and maintains high standards of cuisine and comfort for the parents. There is a crèche run by English nannies split into a soft play and a games and creative play area. There are opportunities to enjoy a wide variety of sports and activities including white water rafting, rock climbing, summer tobogganing, accrobranche (tree-line assault course), quad-biking and grass karting. **Check out page 78.**

Disneyland® Paris, *www.disneylandparis.com 08705 030302.*
A short break here is a magical experience for children of all ages. At Disneyland Park, see your favourite Disney characters at the daily parades, go to Fantasyland where classic Disney fairytales become reality, or enjoy an intergalactic adventure with Space Mountain and its unique sensations. Take a look at how movies are made at the Walt Disney Studios Park and see the characters come to life. Currently, Disney offer 2, 3 or 4 night breaks with an extra night and day free! Selected dates apply. For details or to book call the number above and quote code DSA, or visit the website. **Check out page 76.**

Thomson Al Fresco, *www.thomsonalfresco.co.uk 0870 166 0366.*
Outdoor family fun begins here, with holidays created especially with families in mind. Stay in a luxury, self-catering mobile home in a child-friendly environment at over 40 fun-filled holiday parcs throughout France, Italy, Spain, Portugal and Holland. Every parc has a fantastic range of facilities geared towards the whole family including impressive pool complexes and fun-filled outdoor activities, as well as beautiful beach and lakeside locations. Al Fresco children's clubs provide fun daytime activities for all 4-12 year olds. Choose any date, duration and mode of travel for complete flexibility and with at least one Al Fresco rep resident on-site, there is always help at hand. **Check out page 78.**

Checking for meningitis

In Association with **British Red Cross**

On returning from a family day out, you notice that your son has a rash. How can you tell whether it's meningitis or just a harmless rash?

Place a glass tumbler on the rash and apply pressure. In most cases, this will cause the rash to disappear. However, in the case of meningitis it will remain. Other signs and symptoms include: vomiting, headache, a red or purple rash, stiffness in the neck and pain in the eyes due to light.

If you suspect meningitis, or are in any doubt, seek urgent medical attention.

To learn more about first aid visit redcross.org.uk/firstaid or call 0870 170 9222

COMPETITION

England...
one big
playground!

England is a glorious place for everyone - children all ages! For all the latest events, news and information on what to do here go to **enjoyEngland.com** (the official tourist board website for England).

Order your Enjoy England Great Ideas 2006 brochure
Call: 0845 456 8707
Text: GO to 84118

enjoy**England**.com™

LEGOLAND® WINDSOR

OPEN
31 MARCH - 29 OCTOBER
2006

At LEGOLAND® Windsor the entertainment is certainly hands-on.

Children aged 2-12 years can take to the road, soar through the skies and sail the seas in complete safety. With over 50 interactive rides, live shows, building workshops, driving schools and attractions, all set in 150 acres of beautiful parkland, LEGOLAND Windsor is a different sort of family theme park.

For more information or to book visit **www.LEGOLAND.co.uk**

Places to go outside the area

Visit some exciting places in other counties too.

BERKSHIRE

Windsor, LEGOLAND® Windsor, *www.LEGOLAND.co.uk*
For a fun and exciting day out, head for LEGOLAND Windsor and enjoy over 50 interactive attractions, rides and live shows that will keep the whole family entertained. All set in 150 acres of beautiful parkland and featuring over 47 million LEGO® bricks, it's more fun than you can imagine for children aged 2-12 and their families. Go wild on the Dino Safari, take a spin on the Dino Dipper or enrol your family at the Fire Academy for some active fun! You can also ride the thrilling Jungle Coaster, get behind the wheel at one of the driving schools, pan for pirate gold, brave the Pirate Falls log flume or explore Miniland made from millions of LEGO® bricks. Open 31st Mar-29th Oct 2006, daily (except some Tues & Wed in Spring & Autumn) from 10am, closing times vary. Schools Refreshments V Price G **Check out page 80.**

DERBYSHIRE

Chapel-en-le-Frith(near), Chestnut Centre, Otter, Owl & Wildlife Park,
www.ottersandowls.co.uk 01298 814099.
Situated in an attractive area of the Peak District National Park this is an acknowledged centre for breeding, care and rehabilitation of wild animals. Otters are of particular concern here and every year otter cubs are raised for release into the wild. Display boards help to interpret the countryside scene and there are various specially designed enclosures with otters, wildcats, foxes, owls, polecats and deer. Follow a one-mile nature trail through field and woodlands. A conservation club for 4-11 year olds meets regularly in the Education Centre. The club provides up to date information on all the creatures. You will need at least one and a half hours to see everything. Open daily, Feb Half Term-beginning of Jan (weekends only in Jan/start Feb), 10.30am-5.30pm (dusk in Winter). Schools Birthdays Refreshments **Open all year** Price B **Check out page 82.**

SUSSEX

Cambridge Language & Activity Courses. CLAC, *www.clac.org.uk 01223 240340.*
Interesting summer courses for 8-13 and 13-17 year olds held at two separate sites in lovely countryside locations, Lavant House and Slindon College, West Sussex. The idea is to bring together British and foreign students to create natural language exchange in a motivated and fun environment. There are French, German and Spanish classes for British students and English for overseas students. Fully supervised in a safe environment, there are lots of activities such as swimming, tennis, team games and competitions, drama and music, in addition to the language tuition. Residential or not, these courses offer enjoyable multi-activity weeks with 20 hours of specific tuition in small groups. Courses run weekly during July and August. Please call for more details and a brochure. Birthdays **Check out page 82.**

YORKSHIRE

Skipton, Skipton Castle, *www.skiptoncastle.co.uk 01756 792442.*
This 900 year old fortress standing at the top of Skipton's main street is considered to be one of the most complete medieval castles in England and is fully accessible for children to explore. Visit the castle kitchen and banqueting hall and imagine life living and working in the castle. Children will be fascinated by the dungeons and ancient toilet arrangements! Fun self-guiding tour sheets in a choice of languages, quiz and picnic area available. Check the website for pre-visit children's activities - make a cut-out model or face mask. Open daily, 10am-6pm, Sun from 12noon, Oct-Feb till 4pm. Schools Refreshments **Open all year** Price B **Check out page 84.**

Index

free
Castle Explorer's badge
for under 18's

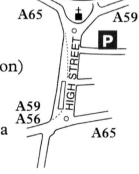

Come & explore
Skipton Castle

Guardian of the gateway to the
Yorkshire Dales for over 900 years.
This unique fortress is one of the
most complete and well-preserved
medieval castles in England.

Open every day from 10am(Sun 12noon)
Last admissions at 6pm (Oct-Feb 4pm)
Free tour sheets in 9 languages.
Family tickets, Tearoom, Shop, Picnic Area
High Street - large carpark nearby
Enquiries: **01756 792442**

A65   A59

A59
A56

A65

www.skiptoncastle.co.uk

Terms & Conditions:

* Not to be used with any other offer.
* No cash alternative.
* Photocopied vouchers are not accepted.
* Voucher is not for re-sale.
* Valid until December 2006.
* Not redeemable against activities.

Terms & Conditions:

* Not to be used with any other offer.
* No cash alternative.
* Photocopied vouchers are not accepted.
* Voucher is not for re-sale.
* Valid until end of 2006 season.

Terms & Conditions:

* 1 individual free with one full paying adult (12yrs and over) paying the full day rate
* Call 0870 999 6680 and quote 'Let's Go Guides'. Tickets are only available when booked in advance and must be booked at least 48 hours prior to your visit
* Not to be used with any other offer
* No cash alternative
* Photocopied vouchers are not accepted
* Voucher is not for re-sale
* Valid until end of 2006 season
* Please check www.chessington.co.uk prior to visit for open and close dates and further information

Terms & Conditions:

* This voucher entitles a maximum of five people to £5.00 off the full admission price per person at LEGOLAND Windsor.
* Entrance for children under three years of age is free.
* Voucher must be presented upon entrance into LEGOLAND Windsor and surrendered to the ticket booth operator. Discount vouchers cannot be pre-booked.
* Not to be used in conjunction with any other offer, reward/loyalty program, 2 Day Pass, Annual Pass, group booking, on-line tickets, rail inclusive offers or an exclusive event or concert.
* Guests are advised that not all attractions and shows may be operational on the day of their visit.
* Height, age and weight restrictions apply on some rides. Some rides will require guests who only just meet the minimum height requirements to be accompanied by a person aged 18 years or over.
* Guests under the age of 14 must be accompanied by a person aged 18 or over.
* This voucher is not for re-sale, is non-refundable and non-transferable.
* The park opens for the 2006 season on 31 March and closes on 29 October 2006.
* This voucher is valid for admissions from 31 March to 29 October 2006 excluding the month of August and selected dates - please check www.LEGOLAND.co.uk in advance to confirm excluded dates.
* This offer is limited to one per household.
* This offer will apply irrespective of the entrance price at the time of use.
* LEGOLAND Windsor will be closed on selected weekdays in March, April, May, September and October.
* PLEASE visit www.LEGOLAND.co.uk in advance to confirm dates and prices.
LEGO, the LEGO logo, LEGOLAND and the LEGOLAND logo are trademarks of the LEGO Group. ©2006 The LEGO Group.